Tino

What people are saying about...

Book—Long Does

Living Prayer

"If effective prayer is your goal, then you'll want to read this book."

> —**Dave Butts,** chairman, National Prayer Committee; president, Harvest
> Prayer Ministries

"I love *Living Prayer* because it reminds me afresh that the treasures waiting to be unearthed in the Word of God are inexhaustible. These pages are filled with the harvest of Dennis Fuqua's tenacious pursuit of more in the place of prayer, offering clear evidence that God *will* be found by those who 'seek Him with all their heart.' And wonderfully, Dennis tells us, he's only scratched the surface!"

> —**Lisa Otis,** ASK Network and The Sentinel Group

"Let Dennis Fuqua take you on a journey with Christ and to Christ through this prayer Christ gave to His church. The journey is strengthened by a glimpse into the author's own walk with the Lord, a walk many of us enjoy with Dennis on our way to the summit of prayer. He has given us not only a book about prayer, but also a prayer book for those who want to walk and talk with our Father in heaven."

> —**Phil Miglioratti,** president, National Pastors' Prayer Network;
> national coordinator, Loving Our Communities to Christ

"Another book on prayer? That was my first thought as I looked at *Living Prayer: The Lord's Prayer Alive in You* by Dennis Fuqua. Then I began to read. I am so thankful for this book. Fresh insights into old words and phrases. If you've never studied the Lord's Prayer, you need to read this book. If you've studied the Lord's Prayer many times, you really need to read this book."

—**Dr. Dan R. Crawford,** senior professor of evangelism and missions, chair of prayer and spiritual formation emeritus, Southwestern Baptist Theological Seminary

"For years I have used the prayer Jesus taught His disciples as the basis for my morning prayer time. Those times have been rich. But thanks to Dennis Fuqua, they should be even richer in the days ahead. I believe that this book can help me and every reader to deepen and enrich our prayer lives. I commend it to you!"

—**Dr. Paul Cedar,** chairman, Mission America Coalition

"I am thrilled that Dennis Fuqua has written this book for at least three reasons: (1) The Lord's Prayer pattern is after all the prototype for all true prayer; (2) Dennis Fuqua is the real deal—when he speaks I listen; (3) I had the privilege of hearing Dennis teach this material to our students at the College of Prayer. Their lives were transformed. Yours will be as well."

—**Fred A. Hartley III,** lead pastor, Lilburn Alliance Church; president, College of Prayer International

"If you had a medical need, you would want a well-educated and highly experienced doctor. If you want to learn to pray, this resource is an outstanding choice. Dennis Fuqua is well-studied and eminently experienced in the dynamics of biblical, balanced prayer. Read and be blessed."

—**Daniel Henderson,** president, Strategic Renewal

"It is amazing how many of us—and I do mean 'us' because I'm certainly included here—have perused the Lord's Prayer, then moved on to what we thought were 'deeper truths' concerning prayer. Dennis does us all a great service by taking us back where we belong, reminding us that when Jesus' disciples asked Him to teach them to pray, His response was both profound and timeless."

—**Mike Higgs,** founder and president, Sondance

"This book made a difference in my prayer life from the day I read it. Dennis Fuqua brings a wealth of personal experience, as well as rich practical and theological insights, to this important topic. He unpacks this best-of-all-prayers by 'the best Pray-er who ever lived' in a fresh and meaningful way. I predict that reading it will draw you to your knees."

—**Dr. Alvin J. VanderGriend,** prayer evangelism associate, Harvest Prayer Ministries

Living Prayer: The Lord's Prayer Alive in You, by my friend and colleague, Dennis Fuqua, is a powerful study on the most foundational prayer of the Christian faith. It has the potential to be so much more than a series of verses we memorize or recite. No matter how well you think you know the Lord's Prayer, there is always more to learn. Dennis will take you on an in-depth journey through Jesus' teaching that has the potential to lead to a renewed faith, spiritual power, and a deeper connection to the heart of God.

—**Kevin Palau,** president, Luis Palau Association

Even for someone like me who has studied this prayer for decades, I still learned a lot and gained new insights as I worked through (*Living Prayer*) the past couple of weeks in my personal quiet time. So readable. So personable. So motivational. So insightful. So beautifully focused on Christ.

—**David Bryant**, founder, Concerts of Prayer and Proclaim Hope!

Everything God wants us to pray for is contained in the Lord's prayer. Dennis does a stellar job of opening this prayer for consumption by those of us who want to learn how to better connect to God with honesty, authenticity, and frequency.

—**Eric Swanson,** missional specialist, Leadership Network

LIVING PRAYER

LIVING PRAYER

The Lord's Prayer
Alive *in* You

DENNIS FUQUA

LIVING PRAYER
© 2012 by Dennis Fuqua
www.livingprayer.net

Published by
Deep River Books
Sisters, Oregon
http://www.deepriverbooks.com

International Standard Book Number: 978-1-61658-027-8
13-digit ISBN: 9781935265993
10-digit ISBN: 1935265997
Library of Congress#: 2011943791

1st edition ©2010 in association with D.C. Jacobson & Associates, LLC.

Edited by Thomas Womack

Printed in the United States of America

Cover design by Kristin Paul Design

Contents

Your Best Invitation

What could possibly compare with being invited into real, heart-to-heart communication with the living and loving God?

Since that's the primary goal of this book, I humbly suggest that this invitation to let the Lord's Prayer live in you is one of the best you'll ever receive.

It isn't a summons to more discipline or ritual; nor are you being invited to a program or formula. Actually, this isn't even an invitation to read a book!

You're being invited to…

- explore one of life's greatest privileges and mysteries.
- learn from the Master about a divine pattern of prayer—and the Person who gave it.
- let words that are common become words that create communion.
- move toward a level of relationship with the Lord that you've known was possible, though it seemed just out of reach.
- take Jesus' words seriously and watch them change your life.
- move from "I *have* to pray" to "I *get* to pray."

To Eat and Drink and Never Be Full

Ultimately, this book is an invitation into a journey, one I've been on since the early 1980s. This path of letting the Lord's Prayer be alive in me has been the greatest impetus to spiritual growth I've ever known, guiding and energizing me while pastoring a congregation and leading a prayer ministry.

Your path and mine won't be exactly the same in this journey. Our steps and vistas will be different because the Word we're dealing with is not only written[1] but also *living*[2]. Yet the destination awaiting us will be the same—a deeper love relationship with Jesus.[3] As you read, I invite

> The Word we're dealing with is not only written but also *living*.

you to listen for Him. His words are far more important than those written here. Listen for the voice of the Master, the real Rabbi, the Good Shepherd. He knows what to say to each of us individually when we ask Him to "teach us to pray." He has promised that you'll hear His voice and follow[4] if you've committed yourself to live for Him. (If you haven't made that commitment, I encourage you to do so right now. You won't regret it!)

This isn't a new journey; others have taken it long before. Sixteen centuries ago, Augustine wrote, "Whatever else we say when we pray, if we pray as we should, we are only saying what is already contained in the Lord's Prayer." Eight centuries later, Thomas Aquinas spoke of the Lord's Prayer as "the most perfect prayer we can say."

Five hundred years ago, Martin Luther walked on this journey. He wrote, "A Christian has prayed abundantly who has

---

1. **Hebrews 4:12,** For the word of God is living and active. Sharper than any double-edged sword, it penetrates even to dividing soul and spirit, joints and marrow; it judges the thoughts and attitudes of the heart.

2. **John 1:14,** The Word became flesh and made his dwelling among us, We have seen his glory, the glory of the One and Only, who came from the Father, full of grace and truth.

3. **James 4:8,** Come near to God and he will come near to you.

4. **John 10:27,** "My sheep listen to my voice; I know them, and they follow me."

rightly prayed the Lord's Prayer." He called it the "model prayer of Christianity," and added,

> To this day I suckle at the Lord's Prayer like a child, and as an old man eat and drink from it and never get my fill. It is the very best prayer.

Modern saints are taking this journey as well. "The Lord's Prayer includes everything you need to ask when you talk to God," writes Elmer Towns, prolific author and a leader in higher Christian education in America. "It is a model prayer that teaches us how to pray." Likewise, Dr. David Cho, pastor in Korea of the world's largest church, affirms that the Lord's Prayer "contains every requirement for which a Christian may pray each day."

Esteemed theologian J. I. Packer declares:

> This prayer is a pattern for all Christian praying. Jesus is teaching that prayer will be acceptable when, and only when, the attitudes, thoughts, and desires expressed fit this pattern. That is to say: every prayer of ours should be a praying of the Lord's Prayer in some shape or form.

"We never get beyond this prayer," Packer continues. "Not only is it the Lord's first lesson in praying, it is all the other lessons too."

Are you learning these lessons from the Lord's Prayer? Are you regularly using this pattern from the Lord Himself for your prayers? This prayer is *His* idea, *His* instruction, and *His* desire for you—and *His* personal invitation.

My hope is that you'll respond to it wholeheartedly…and encourage others to do the same. Are you ready? Let's begin.

PART ONE
This Way In

This section will introduce you to this prayer and explain why and how it can be so helpful to your prayer life.

1. Teach *Me* to Pray—This chapter tells my story of how this prayer became so important to me and how it has shaped my life.

2. Meditating on the Prayer—This chapter explains not only what biblical meditation is, but also how it is an essential activity of learning from Jesus how to pray in this way.

3. The Essence Unlimited—This chapter introduces the prayer by looking at an overview including the focus and structure of the two halves of the prayer.

I have put most of the verses I refer to in this book in footnotes rather than endnotes so it is easier for you to read them as you come to them. I encourage you to refer to them as you read. What they say is more important than what I say about them.

I am aware that many people refer to this prayer as the disciple's prayer rather than the Lord's Prayer and refer to John 17 as the Lord's Prayer. I have no argument with this distinction but have chosen to refer to this prayer as the Lord's Prayer because that is the way most people think of this section of Scripture.

I offer you the following translation of the Lord's Prayer as one to memorize and meditate on as we move through the rest of this study:

Our Father in heaven,

let Your name be holy,

let Your kingdom come,

and let Your will be done

on earth as it is in heaven.

Give us today our daily bread.

Forgive us our debts as we forgive our debtors.

Lead us not into temptation,

but deliver us from the evil one.

(Optional: for the kingdom and the power

and the glory belong to You!)

Amen!

(Matthew 6:9–13, author's translation)

Chapter 1
Teach Me to Pray

It came like a download from God—countless megabytes per second (though at the time I didn't have such words to describe my experience). The message was instantly all there, though it took me a few moments to "read"—and all the days since to grow in living it out.

The message from God was clear—like writing on the wall, but written on the wall of my heart.

I remember the exact moment it happened, one spring day decades ago. I was just stepping out of a borrowed motor home parked on secluded, undeveloped property just off Highway 16 near Gig Harbor, Washington. I was there alone for a few days on a personal spiritual retreat with a specific mission and a specific request to Jesus (though I hadn't used these exact words): "Lord, teach me to pray."

It's not that I'd never given prayer serious attention. I grew up with prayer, and after attending Bible college, then serving as a pastor for four years, I could look back and say that I'd taken an active role in opportunities to pray. I'd attended prayer seminars and conferences. I'd made commitments regarding prayer and mostly fulfilled them. I prayed with and for others, and I tried to make prayer a priority in my life.

But something inside kept telling me, *You need to pray a lot more and a lot better.* I knew I'd only scratched the surface (if that) of this thing called prayer.

So I borrowed my mother's motor home and took it to that secluded area off Highway 16, where I planned to spend two or three days, then come back a more effective pray-er.

I passed the time unhurriedly, sitting and praying, kneeling and praying, walking and praying. I prayed aloud and prayed silently. I read and prayed, and sang and prayed. I deliberately asked God to help me pray better.

It was on my second morning there that I stepped out the motor home door and received God's "download." I still remember the moment; I'd just placed my right foot on the first step down. Crystal-clear thoughts came suddenly to my heart and mind. My level of listening spiked. I had an unmistakable sense that these were not just my thoughts; this was God beginning to answer my request.

His Three-Part Message

Reflecting on what the Lord said, I came to see three parts to it.

First, I sensed His pleasure. "Dennis," He seemed to say, "what you are doing is good. You want to pray better. I want you to pray better too! We are in agreement here."

I understood the seriousness of these words, though they were a bit tongue-in-cheek. He was giving me a pat on the back but also a kick in the pants. I sensed Him telling me that the people in my church deserved a pastor who knew how to pray better than I currently did.

Second, I sensed the Lord's comments along these lines: "You know, you're not the first person to ask Me how to pray. My guys asked me this years ago." Obviously I knew that—but these words still came as a surprise to me. Somehow I thought my request was very novel!

Finally, His punch line: "I gave My guys an answer that, frankly, I thought was pretty good. In fact, I can't think of a better answer for *you*. And if you think you need a different one, I don't have it."

I knew what He meant. If I wanted Him to teach me to pray more effectively, I should "pretend" that the instruction He gave His followers two thousand years ago was still valid today. I should begin letting this prayer become *alive* in me.

His message came across strongly. I even felt that He was saying I should "practice" this for the next fifty years.

Though it hasn't been that long, I can tell you without question that my most effective times of prayer since then have come as I've followed the pattern of this prayer—making the Lord's Prayer my own.

Repeated for a Reason

I immediately began to take this prayer seriously.

I knew it was recorded in two different places in the New Testament—in Matthew 6 and Luke 11. As I turned to them, I learned a significant fact: These passages are not two accounts of the same event but have two different settings and contexts. Matthew and Luke recorded two different occasions when Jesus taught virtually the same thing about prayer. In Matthew, Jesus initiated the topic while He was teaching. In Luke, the disciples initiated the topic after watching Jesus pray—as if they told themselves, "This guy's good at this! Let's ask Him to teach us!"

These two events were separated by many miles and many months. The Matthew account is near Galilee, and the Luke account took place near Jerusalem. Over the years, I've checked this out with several books that harmonize the Gospels. They're all in agreement in listing them as different occasions. For example, Burton Throckmorton, in *Gospel Parallels,* presents an ordered list of 253 events in Jesus' life; the Matthew account of the Lord's Prayer is number 30, while the Luke account is 146.

The point is that the Lord's Prayer isn't something Jesus randomly mentioned, but something fundamental that He deliberately repeated.

If we put these two passages in a modern context, it might look something like this:

In a classroom one day, Jesus brings up the topic of prayer. He tells his pupils clearly how to do it, and they carefully take notes.

Months later, He's giving His students an opportunity to ask questions. One guy raises his hand and asks, "Jesus, would you teach us how to pray?"

With a wry smile He answers, "Yeah, I can do that."

They bring out their notebooks as He begins speaking. A couple of lines into it, their pencils slow down. Soon they aren't writing anymore because what they're hearing is familiar.

As Jesus finishes, there's a moment of silence. One student raises his hand. "Isn't this the same thing You told us a while back?"

Jesus folds His arms across His chest, leans back, and slowly nods. *They got it.*

In Matthew, we have Jesus—the best pray-er ever, the One who invented prayer in the first place, God Himself in human form—telling His followers exactly how He wanted them to pray! He's very clear and specific: "This, then, is how you should pray" (6:9). He was serious about this, as He outlined the pattern of prayer.

Then in Luke, in response to the disciples' question, He's clear again: "When you pray, say..." (11:2). By outlining the same pattern a second time, He communicated to them that He was *really* serious!

They got it.

Finally, I did too.

Learning How

I began, right there in the motor home, by simply kneeling down and praying this prayer aloud, word for word, very slowly. I was in no hurry to get through it. I just wanted to really *get* it and to really mean each word. Still, it took a relatively short time, perhaps less than a minute. I did this several times.

Then the Holy Spirit did something that put me on a whole new track. He began to highlight for me a single word or phrase of the prayer. When He did, I would pause on that word or phrase, thinking and meditating about it, and He would unpack or amplify its meaning for me. Related thoughts and Scriptures would come to my mind, and as they did, I incorporated them into the words of this prayer.

Jesus was teaching me how to pray!

This pattern was established many years ago in that motor home, but it continues to this day in my home.

Soon it wasn't uncommon for me to pray for long periods without getting through the whole prayer. Sometimes I would start in the middle or toward the end. Sometimes I would focus exclusively on one line or even one word of the prayer.

My times of prayer became increasingly creative. I soon became convinced that the Lord is as creative now as He has ever been. We don't have to worry about exhausting His creativity as we pray through this prayer. The governing dynamic is not *our* creativity; it's *His* creativity being expressed to and through us.

The key is to *listen*. Listen to how the Holy Spirit is using this prayer; then speak His words after Him. Listen to His explanation and application of a word or phrase; then pray it back to Him. Listen as He "guide[s] you into all truth," which is one of the Spirit's primary roles in our life.[1]

After praying this prayer many, many times over the years, I can tell you that my most effective times of prayer have been, and still are, when I've followed this pattern. The Lord continually unfolds new things from its lines and thoughts. But I also want you to know that new, creative uses of this prayer is not the goal; the goal is simply using it *now* in a fresh way.

There are many prayers the Lord wants to hear from us again and again. He wants to hear us tell Him we love Him. He wants us to tell Him we're thankful and to ask Him for protection, guidance, and wisdom. Current freshness in prayer is more important than creativity. *Meaning* the words is more important than the words we say.

---

1. **John 16:13,** "But when He the Spirit of truth comes, He will guide you into all truth."

I Won't Insist

I've often pondered the disciples' request in Luke 11:1 "Lord, teach us to pray." If you're not regularly making this same request of the Savior, you're missing a wonderful opportunity to have the Master tutor you in a most needed and delightful skill. Who better to learn from? And how better to learn!

A major purpose of this book will be accomplished if you catch two things right away: (1) Asking Jesus to teach you to pray is one of the most important questions you can ever ask Him. (2) And *when* you ask, His best answer is going to include the same thoughts He included in Matthew 6 and Luke 11.

> **If you're not regularly making this same request of the Savior, you're missing a wonderful opportunity.**

The only thing left for you and me is to just do it.

I'm fully convinced that Jesus really wants you to regularly pray the pattern of this prayer. But I won't insist that you *must* pray in this way. Why?

First, I've found that invitations work better than commands.

Second, this command has already been given to you by One with far more authority than me, and He meant it!

Will you ask Him (again and again) to teach you to pray? Will you make it a regular prayer? Then listen and keep listening. Don't listen for a new answer, but listen to the answer He has already given. Listen to the instructions He has given you in the Lord's Prayer. Listen as He clarifies that message for you in personal terms.

You'll be letting the Lord's Prayer become *alive* in you.

Responding

1. Ask the Lord to teach you to pray, and then listen for His instructions.

2. Pray through the Lord's Prayer slowly a few times, seeking to mean each word.

Chapter 2
Open Our Eyes

About the time the Lord began speaking to me about the value of the Lord's Prayer, I also received more instruction about the importance of biblical meditation. Later, I realized how vitally connected these two truths are. In fact, the Lord's Prayer will become alive in us *only to the degree that we meditate on it*. Without that meditation, we won't be able to pray the way Jesus intended.

So before looking more closely at this prayer, let's clarify some meditation basics.

The value of such interaction with the Scriptures is made especially clear in three passages. Joshua 1:8 says that meditation will lead to obedience, which will in turn lead to prosperity and success.[1] Psalm 1:1–3 teaches that meditation leads us to blessing, fruitfulness, and firmness (a solid foundation).[2] Psalm 119:97&99 shows that meditation reflects our love for His law and gives us great insight and wisdom.[3]

---

1. **Joshua 1:8,** Do not let this Book of the Law depart from your mouth; meditate on it day and night, so that you may be careful to do everything written in it. Then you will be prosperous and successful.

2. **Psalm 1:1–3,** Blessed is the man who does not walk in the counsel of the wicked or stand in the way of sinners or sit in the seat of mockers. But his delight is in the law of the Lord, and on his law he meditates day and night. He is like a tree planted by streams of water, which yields its fruit in season and whose leaf does not wither. Whatever he does prospers.

3. **Psalm 119:97&99,** Oh, how I love your law! I meditate on it all day long.... I have more insight than all my teachers, for I meditate on your statutes.

I think we can say that meditation is *the most important way* we interact with God's Word. We're to read His Word, hear it, study it, and memorize it, but unless we're meditating on it, we aren't deriving all we can from it.

What is scriptural meditation? Well, it is *not* a cleaned up version of what has come out of Eastern religious systems. It's not about emptying our mind to expand our experience. Nor is it about outward things like chanting or sitting in a certain position.

It *is* about filling and flooding our mind with the truth of God's Word in order to hear from Him and expand our capacity for Him.

The Hebrew (Old Testament) word for *meditation* is related to the concepts of reflection, repetition, contemplation, and even murmuring. So in one sense, we already know how to meditate. All we have to do is just murmur and complain a bit, but trade our concerns for the concerns of His Word, and we have a pretty good practice of meditation!

Its meaning also suggests a cow chewing her cud. A cow takes a bite of grass, chews it for a while, and then swallows it. She has received some nourishment from that experience, but she is not finished with the grass yet. What does she do? After the grass is in one stomach for a while, the cow brings it back up, chews it some more, gets more nourishment from it, then swallows it again. For us, biting the food, chewing the food, and tasting the food all may be enjoyable, but it is only as we *swallow* the food that we receive nourishment. The same is true in the spiritual realm. It is only as we swallow (or agree with) the truths of His Word that we receive nourishment. Meditation is spiritual swallowing.

James 1:21, in the King James Version, refers to the "engrafted" word.[4] His Word can be grafted into us. Have you ever grafted a branch onto a tree? It is done so that an ordinary kind of stump (a tough one that has a strong root system but would not normally produce good fruit) can be matched with a branch that has inherently good fruit, with the hope that the combination can produce a good crop. In this illustration, we are the old stump and the Word is the branch.

How do we get the two together? You scrape the stump and the branch to expose bare wood. Then you use an external system (wires, poles, etc.) to hold the branch close to the stump. Then you wrap a cloth around the joint to keep it snug and moist. After the external mechanism has held it in place long enough, it can be removed and the branch will stay put. Soon the fruit that was in the branch all along begins to grow.

The same is true for us. When we use the external system of our minds to intentionally hold a truth of Scripture against our soul and spirit, keeping it moist by God's Spirit, a time will come when we do not need to continue to think about it because it has become part of us. We have thought about it much, sought to see its significance to our situation, and prayed that our lives would be lined up with that truth. That has helped us obey the Scripture, and we will see the fruit of that passage of Scripture take root in our lives.

Three Steps

Just as the end result of all our interaction with the Word should be meditation, so also the end result of meditation should be

---

4. **James 1:21,** And receive with meekness the engrafted word, which is able to save your souls.

prayer. In fact, the final part of meditation *is* prayer. Meditation begins with *pondering* the text, then moves to *personalizing* it, and concludes with *praying* the text back to God. These three steps make up the meditation process.

Pondering cannot be done in a hurry—no microwave, no drive-through window. Pondering means we spend time lingering on each word. We ask questions like these: What does this word mean here and in other places? Why might the author have used this word instead of another? How does it relate to the words before and after it? How might it be stated differently without changing the meaning? The more questions like these we ask, the more observations we make, and the better we understand the word's meaning. We let the truth of it seep deeply into our mind and heart.

Pondering cannot be done in a hurry.

Personalizing means we see the implications of the words to our own lives. "For God so loved the world" in John 3:16 becomes "For God so loved *me...*" We let the Lord change some of the pronouns so that the words relate directly to us and our situation. This process allows the life and the power of God's Word to come off the pages of the Book and into the places of our heart and spirit where it is most needed. It is letting the Author of the Book explain and apply the message of His writing directly to our life. It is hearing God's contemporary commentary on His eternal Word. As we personalize the truth, we allow the Holy Spirit to determine what part of our life needs it; then we press that truth up against us—into our heart and spirit—until it becomes part of us.

I said earlier that the end result of meditation should be prayer. But this middle step of personalization is the apex of meditation. The more we hear from God through meditation, the more effective our prayers will be.

Praying through the text is the last step. Now we direct the truth of the text back to the Lord. "For God so loved me" becomes "For *You* so loved me…" We align our words and heart with what we've heard the Lord say to us.

This is how we chew the Scriptures as a cow chews her cud. This is how we graft the Word into our lives. This is what takes us from understanding to believing and doing, which leads to blessing.

Together at the Table

I find a vivid portrayal of meditation in the account of the resurrected Lord and the two disciples He walked with on the road to Emmaus. As their journey that day ended, their response to Him was appropriate, though they hadn't yet recognized who he really was:

> They urged him strongly, "Stay with us, for it is nearly evening; the day is almost over." So he went in to stay with them. When he was at the table with them, he took bread, gave thanks, broke it and began to give it to them. Then their eyes were opened and they recognized him, and he disappeared from their sight. (Luke 24:29–31)

Notice what these two disciples did:

They *invited Jesus* to come and stay with them.

They *sat with Him* at the table.

They *listened* to His voice.

They *received* the bread He offered.

As a result, "their eyes were opened"; they recognized Him when He revealed Himself to them.

This is how we meditate. We invite Jesus into our setting, listen to His voice, and receive what He offers us. In the process, we get to know Him more and more.

Notice also what Jesus did here: He responded to their request to stay with them, and He sat with them. He took the bread, gave thanks, broke it, and gave it to them. This is what Jesus does when we meditate on His words. What an amazing thought that the Lord of heaven would so respond when we invite Him to stay and share His words with us!

As we meditate on the Lord's Prayer, the benefit will be better prayer *to* Him, better relationship *with* Him, and better representation *of* Him. On the other hand, if we do not take the time to meditate on it, we will not be able to pray it the way Jesus had in mind.

I've shared these thoughts on meditation because the rest of this book has sprung from my own times of meditation on the Lord's Prayer and because any lasting value you receive from this book will come only through your own meditation on this wonderful prayer—as you *ponder, personalize,* and *pray* your way through it.

———◆———

Responding

1. How would you express your own heartfelt desire for what you want the Lord to teach you now about prayer? Make that request to Him now in prayer.

2. Spend some time meditating (pondering, personalizing, and praying) on either one word or one line of the Lord's Prayer.

Chapter 3
The Essence Unlimited

The Lord's Prayer is like a bucket of water drawn from a river; it contains the essence of the thing, but not its full dimensions.

Here in these words of Jesus we find prayer's essence reduced to its minimum—which, when expanded, covers basically all aspects of prayer. Our Lord's words here are absolutely packed with meaning. As we pray them with the help of the Holy Spirit, they really do become unlimited.

Before we look at this prayer word by word and line by line, let's observe its overall structure. We find a salutation followed by seven requests. The requests are clearly divided into two parts. The first half focuses on *God* and *His desires*:

Our Father in heaven,

let Your name be holy,

let Your kingdom come,

and let Your will be done

on earth as it is in heaven.

The second half focuses on *us* and *our needs*:

Give us today our daily bread.

Forgive us our debts as we forgive our debtors.

Lead us not into temptation,

but deliver us from the evil one.

Many prayers can flow from the nouns in the first part and the verbs in the second. Picture the words of this prayer on a computer screen. Each one can become a "hyperlink" to more divine web pages related to it. By "clicking" on these sites, your prayers will become deeper and broader.

Our Father's Desires

The key pronoun of the first half of the prayer is *Your*. God's priorities involve His name, His kingdom, and His will. The King James Version of this prayer uses "Thy" rather than "Your." Can you say "thy" and "my" at the same time? Neither can I. Just as it is not possible to say those two words at the same time, it is also not possible to pray those two thoughts at the same time. I have found that praying "Thy" reduces my desire to pray "my."

Jesus looked first to His Father's concerns. This was always His primary focus, as His later prayer in Gethsemane would demonstrate profoundly: "Not as I will, but as you will" (Matthew 26:39).

This should also be the pattern in our prayers. We place His priorities over ours; we concentrate on what's most important to Him before turning to our own needs or desires.

> **Have you ever heard someone say, "Jesus, what are *Your* prayer requests"?**

You've been in groups of people praying where the key question was, "What are your prayer requests?" Have you ever heard someone say, "Jesus, what are *Your* prayer requests?" If we actually asked that, I believe He would respond, "Thank you for inquiring; not many people do. I have three requests: that My Father's name would be holy, that His kingdom would come, and that His will would be done."

These three requests are seen throughout Scripture. In fact, they provide a good lens for observing all of the Bible. They're clear and all-encompassing, and by getting to know them, we get to know God's heart. Because they're His deep desires, they should also become the deep desires in the hearts of His followers, fully reflected in our prayers.

The Plumb Line

I've found it helpful to "untie" the phrase "on earth as it is in heaven" from the third request ("let Your will be done") so it can be appropriately and equally related to all three of these requests. Just because "Your kingdom come" rhymes with "Your will be done" doesn't mean they're a couplet. The three requests here should be seen together. For all three, heaven is the template, and earth is the target.

I believe this is an appropriate view because heaven is mentioned immediately before and immediately after these three requests. This helps us see all three as a unit and also helps us recognize that we look toward heaven to learn how to craft our prayers.

More importantly, the verb form of all three requests is the same in the original language. We might even read them this way: "Name, be holy. Kingdom, come. Will, be done."

With a little thought, it becomes obvious that *in heaven* God's name is already quite holy; His kingdom has definitely come there; and His will is assuredly accomplished there. The point in Jesus' words is that these three things have *not* been fully accomplished here on earth. *This* is where those prayers need to be answered.

Heaven is the plumb line of this prayer and all prayers. In heaven, these things are already the way they're supposed to be. Heaven is the standard. Our prayers are to make copies of those heavenly things and distribute them here on earth. Praying is joining God in the process of getting heaven from there to here through us.

So the three requests look like this:

Let Your name be holy
Let Your kingdom come } on earth as it is in heaven.
Let Your will be done

I invite you to pray through this first half of the Lord's Prayer in this manner:

Father, let Your name be holy here on earth, just as it is in heaven.

Let Your kingdom come here on earth, just as it has come in heaven.

And let Your will be done here on earth, just as it's being done in heaven.

Initially, we may not understand all of what we're asking, but as we meditate and keep praying, the Holy Spirit will give us more understanding.

Our Needs

In the prayer's second half, the verbs help us grasp the flow: *Give us. Forgive us. Lead us (not).* And *deliver us.*

These verbs include nearly all the requests we might have in life. We need provision. We need forgiveness, and to grant forgiveness. We need leadership. And we need deliverance.

Again, countless hours of prayer material are contained in

these short little phrases. Consider what they reveal about who God is. He is a giver, a forgiver, a leader, a deliverer. Even if that were all we knew of Him, it would still be wonderful, wouldn't it?

Now consider what these verbs reveal about us and our situation. They tell us we have both physical and nonphysical needs that only He can supply. Specifically, we have a continuing need both to receive and grant forgiveness. Also, we do best when we follow His leadership. And when we fail at that, we certainly need His deliverance.

Changing Profiles

Part of this prayer's purpose is to produce change in us. As we continually pray these requests, we're transformed. We develop a desire not simply to pray this prayer, but to *be* this prayer. It remakes us into a certain kind of person:

- You marvel that you're a child of God.
- You deeply revere His name.
- You long for His kingdom.
- You delight to do His will.
- You're utterly dependent on God for all your needs.
- You're keenly aware of your deep need for forgiveness.
- You understand that extending forgiveness is not a "have to" but a "get to."
- You desperately need and want God's leadership.
- You know you need and want His deliverance.
- You rest assuredly in God's position, ability, and reputation.

As we continue praying in this manner, we also become more

aware of who our Father really is. We develop in our hearts a more accurate profile of the One to whom we pray:

- He's our Father.
- He is "heavenly."
- He greatly values His name.
- He rules His kingdom.
- He accomplishes His will.
- He provides our needs as our sufficient Source.
- He's able and willing to forgive us.
- He calls us to forgive as He forgives.
- He's able and willing to lead us.
- He's able and willing to deliver us.

Helpful Patterns

So what we have in the first half of this prayer is an earthly child agreeing with His heavenly Father about wanting to see heaven reflected on earth in three specific ways—that His name would be revealed and revered, His kingdom be established and expanded, and His will be understood and accomplished.

And in the prayer's second half, we have a child who needs provision looking to his Father as the Great Source of provision; a child who needs forgiveness looking to his Father as the Great Forgiver; a child who needs leadership looking to his Father as the Great Leader; and a child who needs deliverance looking to his Father as the Great Deliverer.

Jesus shows us another relationship between the two halves of the prayer again only a few verses after He gives us this prayer. In Matthew 6:33, Jesus says, "But seek first His kingdom and His righteousness, and all these things will be given to you as well." Since Jesus is calling us to set God's kingdom as our first priority, it is not too much to see the other two requests from the first half of this prayer (regarding His name and His will) as just as important. When we do this, all the other things we need (summarized in the second half of the prayer) will be taken care of as well. We need Him to provide for us, to forgive us, to lead us, and to deliver us. So when we make His priorities our prayer priorities, He makes our needs His priorities.

When we make His priorities our prayer priorities, He makes our needs His priorities.

Praying in this manner brings our lives more in line with God's will as revealed in this prayer and our thinking more in line with the God who is revealed in this prayer.

———◆———

Responding

1. *Which noun from the prayer's first half (God's name, kingdom, will) or verb from the prayer's second half (give, forgive, lead, deliver) has shown you the most about who God is? Speak or write to the Lord a prayer around that one word.*

2. *Pray through one of the profiles expressing either thanks to God for who He is or your desire to become more of what this prayer reflects.*

3. *Pray through some of the prayers from part 3 beginning on page 153 that relate to the whole prayer (1–16).*

Part Two
Understanding the Prayer

If we are to pray this prayer effectively, we need a basic understanding of what each line means. The chapters in this section are not an exhaustive study of each line, but they will give you enough understanding to pray through the Lord's Prayer with confidence and clarity.

Chapter 4
"Our Father in Heaven..."

It was dark that morning, not only when we drove up the mountain, but also later as we came back down. I was in Tucson, Arizona, as the guest of my friend Pat, a pastor. I was there to share the vision of what God can do in a city when pastors come together for extended prayer. For a couple of days, we had met with several pastors individually and in groups. We had been interviewed on Christian radio. We'd eaten, talked, and laughed together.

Now Pat and I prayed together over this city.

Pat grew up in Tucson, and the church he pastors there is one he planted twenty years earlier. He cares deeply about the welfare of his city. A few years ago, God called him to begin meeting Him on that mountain at 4:30 each morning for prayer. I'd heard him mention this prayer time, so when he invited me to join him, the opportunity was too good to pass up. He picked me up in his Jeep and drove us to a viewpoint, five thousand feet in elevation, overlooking Tucson.

As we sat at the viewpoint and looked down on the city lights, we began praying through the pattern of the Lord's Prayer. Though we prayed through many parts of the prayer, I got stuck on *our*. *Our* Father, give *us*, forgive *us*, lead *us*, deliver *us*. This wasn't just *my* prayer; it was *our* prayer. Pat and I prayed in agreement. And as we prayed, I sensed a clear connection not only with him, but with the other local pastors we'd spent time with who also cared about the city. From our vantage point on the mountain, I could see the areas where we'd met these men, and I pictured us praying with them. That grew to include other pastors in town who shared the same burden. Soon it expanded to all the believers in Tucson who loved the Lord and their city.

My prayers were better because they weren't just mine. *We* were praying to *our* Father.

Our

The first thing Jesus teaches us in this wonderful model prayer is the value of praying in the plural. He begins not with *My* Father, but *our* Father. He continues throughout the prayer using *us* and *our*.

Though this prayer can certainly be prayed by an individual, its primary application seems to be for groups. In fact, much of the New Testament discussion of prayer assumes that it's a corporate activity (as in Acts 2:42; 4:23–26; 12:12; Colossians 1:3–4; 1:9–14; 4:2–4).[1]

---

1. **Acts 2:42,** They devoted themselves to the apostles' teaching and to the fellowship, to the breaking of bread and to prayer.

   Acts 4:23–26, On their release, Peter and John went back to their own people and reported all that the chief priests and elders had said to them. When they heard this, they raised their voices together in prayer to God. "Sovereign Lord," they said, "you made the heaven and the earth and the sea, and everything in them. You spoke by the Holy Spirit through the mouth of your servant, our father David: "'Why do the nations rage and the peoples plot in vain? The kings of the earth take their stand and the rulers gather together against the Lord and against his Anointed One.'"

   Acts 12:12, When this had dawned on him, he went to the house of Mary the mother of John, also called Mark, where many people had gathered and were praying.

   Colossians 1:3–4, We always thank God, the Father of our Lord Jesus Christ, when we pray for you, 4 because we have heard of your faith in Christ Jesus and of the love you have for all the saints.

   Colossians 1:9–14, For this reason, since the day we heard about you, we have not stopped praying for you and asking God to fill you with the knowledge of his will through all spiritual wisdom and understanding. And we pray this in order that you may live a life worthy of the

Paul's command to "pray without ceasing" (1 Thessalonians 5:17) was written not to an individual, but to a congregation. And when Jesus instructs His disciples about prayer in Matthew 18:19[2], the Greek word translated as *agree* is one from which we get our word *symphony*. It's hard to be a symphony all by yourself! That picture should teach us that we each have a part to play: Sometimes I'm playing (and praying) with others; sometimes I'm simply enjoying and agreeing with their prayers. It should also remind us to all be reading from the same music and following the same Conductor. Praying in concert with others is powerful.

What you read and learn in this book applies both to individual and group prayer. In fact, as your personal prayer life grows, you'll be better able to contribute to group prayer, and as your corporate prayer life grows, you'll enter into deeper personal prayer.

Individual prayer is, of course, very valuable. Many times Jesus got alone to pray[3]. But corporate prayer can be a fuller experience than individual prayer. Corporate prayer allows us to hear the heart of the one praying as he or she speaks to God (while we listen in) rather than to us. It also allows us to hear God's heart through the prayers of another.

Lord and may please him in every way: bearing fruit in every good work, growing in the knowledge of God, being strengthened with all power according to his glorious might so that you may have great endurance and patience, and joyfully giving thanks to the Father, who has qualified you to share in the inheritance of the saints in the kingdom of light. For he has rescued us from the dominion of darkness and brought us into the kingdom of the Son he loves, in whom we have redemption, the forgiveness of sins.

Colossians 4:2–4, Devote yourselves to prayer, being watchful and thankful. And pray for us, too, that God may open a door for our message, so that we may proclaim the mystery of Christ, for which I am in chains. Pray that I may proclaim it clearly, as I should.

2. Matthew 18:19, "Again, I tell you that if two of you on earth agree about anything you ask for, it will be done for you by my Father in heaven."

3. Luke 5:16, But Jesus often withdrew to lonely places and prayed.

Marilyn and I often prayed together while we were engaged. One day after a time of prayer in a park near the school we attended, I realized that as I listened to her pray, I'd learned more of her heart than if we'd spent a much longer time just talking.

As we pray with others, we hear another perspective based on a different history, personality, situation, and theology. It helps us pray "off of" one another's prayers; our prayers end up being deeper and better because we've used each other's prayers to help launch our own. It also allows us to exercise the biblical action of agreement (saying "Amen").

Corporate prayer is beneficial not only to us, but also to God. He likes harmony. He likes agreement. In Psalm 133:3[4], there's a commanded blessing awaiting groups who come to Him in genuine unity. In Revelation 5:8[5], God likens the prayers of the saints (in the plural) to incense that rises before Him. As we pray together, we each bring different ingredients needed for the full fragrance. God likes the smell of our prayers mixed together and rising up before His throne. The end result of corporate prayer is that Jesus hears one prayer through many voices rather than many different prayers.

> **As we pray together, we each bring different ingredients needed for the full fragrance.**

I deeply appreciate the many opportunities I have had to facilitate Prayer Summits. Through them I have come to greatly appre-

---

4. **Psalm 133:3,** For there the Lord commanded the blessing, even life for evermore. (KJV)

5. **Revelation 5:8,** And when he had taken it, the four living creatures and the twenty-four elders fell down before the Lamb. Each one had a harp and they were holding golden bowls full of incense, which are the prayers of the saints.

ciate the power of corporate prayer. The depth of my worship of and wonder for God is deeper because I have prayed with others.

One morning, as I was facilitating a Prayer Summit for pastors in the Treasure Valley (Boise, Idaho) area, someone sang the song "Turn Your Eyes upon Jesus." I could not count how many times I have sung that song. But this time as we sang, the words "Look full in His wonderful face" stood out to me like they were marked with a yellow highlighter. So when we finished the song, I simply said, "Men, we just sang the words 'Look full in His wonderful face.' Let's just take some time and do that. Let's look at Jesus' face and simply pray back to Him what we see." It was one of those times when God was obviously present.

The next thirty to forty-five minutes was one of the deepest times of worship I have experienced in a long time. One man described an aspect of God's compassion seen in Jesus' eyes. Another spoke to God about the scars on Jesus' face and the brutality He experienced in the process of purchasing our salvation. Another referenced His facial features at different stages in Jesus' life. It continued on and on with pastors pouring out their love and appreciation of the Savior. The power of this time was not simply that any one of us was gazing at and glorifying God, but that we were able to "build upon" one another's statements of praise. The sum of the united prayers was more than the sum of the individual prayers.

But we can also pray "in the plural" even when we're not actually with other people. This word *our* fits any group of which we're a part, as we pray for them—family, community, congregation, company, or country.

Often when I'm praying by myself, I pray for "*our* family" rather than "*my* family." I've found that it equalizes my praying. My prayers are more inclusive and therefore less self-centered. Seeing myself as part of a group, even when I'm praying by myself, gives me a better and broader perspective, allowing me to better sense the needs and priorities of others. I bring others before the Lord in a way that lines up more with the way things really are.

This word *our* also reminds us that we're part of the body of Christ. Since many different people call Him "Our Father," if they're part of God's family, they're part of my family, even though they come from different cultures, different languages, different geographies, different priorities, different theological persuasions, different histories, and different styles. Praying with the word *our* should remind us that we're connected with all true believers everywhere and for all time—with every person who has ever known God as their Father.

Father

God has many titles. He's the Door, the Shepherd, the Healer, the Provider, and more. In fact, "God" isn't really His name but His primary title. It means "strong one." And "Holy" isn't the Holy Spirit's first name but rather His most prominent characteristic.

Think of some of the titles that actually and accurately describe our God: He's the Creator. He's the Holy One of Israel. He's the Almighty God, Captain of the hosts of heaven.

Knowing all this, when Jesus taught us how to pray, He told us to use a very personal, relational term. It would have been accurate and appropriate for Him to say, "Begin by bowing low and recognizing that you're coming to the high and lofty One, the Most Holy God of the entire universe, the all-knowing and all-powerful Creator and King!" But instead Jesus told us to come and call God "Papa," just as He did. Though we should never come casually, our approach should be as comfortable as a child coming to his or her daddy. Think of it—access to the God of heaven is more inviting than access to the best possible earthly father.

Can you appreciate the risk Jesus took in telling us to address God as our *Father*? Though all fathers are supposed to reflect the character of our wonderful heavenly Father, Jesus knew that none would do so perfectly. He knew that the best father in this world is only a marred reflection of our awesome heavenly Father. And He also knew that some of us would have fathers who were so far from reflecting His character that they would distort His image to the point of being unrecognizable. But Jesus also knew that no matter how inaccurately our fathers reflected His Father, there are certain things we can know about His Father simply from the inherent concept of fatherhood.

Your father, no matter how he acted toward you, taught you about the heavenly Father. Sometimes it was by way of comparison, and sometimes it was by way of contrast, but either way, our earthly dads have taught us much about our heavenly Father. So if your earthly father did a great job, don't settle for that level of awareness of your heavenly Father. And if your earthly father did a very poor job, don't let that limit you from experiencing deep relationship with the best Father ever!

Jesus often referred to God as His Father. It's the most common way He began His prayers. For example, in His passionate prayer in John 17, notice how Jesus addresses God, as well as the particular requests associated with this approach:

Father, the time has come. Glorify your Son, that your Son may glorify you....

And now, *Father, glorify me* in your presence with the glory I had with you before the world began....

I will remain in the world no longer, but they are still in the world, and I am coming to you. *Holy Father, protect them* by the power of your name—the name you gave me—so that they may be one as we are one....

...*that all of them may be one, Father,* just as you are in me and I am in you. *May they also be in us* so that the world may believe that you have sent me....

Father, I want those you have given me to be with me where I am, and to see my glory, the glory you have given me because you loved me before the creation of the world. *Righteous Father,* though the world does not know you, *I know you,* and they know that you have sent me. (John 17:1, 5, 11, 21, 24–25)

And also in Gethsemane:

My Father, if it is possible, *may this cup be taken from me.* Yet not as I will, but as you will. (Matthew 26:39)

And especially on the cross:

Father, forgive them, for they do not know what they are doing.…
Father, into your hands I commit my spirit. (Luke 23:34, 46)

At these crucial points in His life, Jesus was especially aware of being the Son of His Father.

The Father also addressed Jesus as "Son" on at least two occasions, when He actually spoke out of heaven and affirmed, "This is My beloved Son" (Matthew 3:17; 17:5, KJV).

Here's the point: The closest and most meaningful, important, and significant relationship in the entire universe is between the Father and the Son—and *this is the relationship that we, as His children, have been invited into.* This is the relationship that forms the basis for and the direction of the Lord's Prayer and our prayers.

Furthermore, since we're to call God "Father" as Jesus does, it means I can call Jesus my Brother! He's not ashamed to be known as our Brother.[6] At times, we've given good reason for even our earthly brothers and sisters to be ashamed of us, never mind Jesus. Yet He's very clear that we, as sons and daughters of God, are accepted by Jesus as His siblings.

Calling God our "Father" also implies a sharing in His nature. We read in John 5:18[7] that one reason the Jewish leaders wanted to kill Jesus was because He called God His Father. In their minds,

6. **Hebrews 2:11,** Both the one who makes men holy and those who are made holy are of the same family. So Jesus is not ashamed to call them brothers.

7. **John 5:18,** For this reason the Jews tried all the harder to kill him; not only was he breaking the Sabbath, but he was even calling God his own Father, making himself equal with God.

this was a claim of equality with God. Their understanding of a father/son relationship was far more profound than ours today; they saw it as something ascribing the father's character to the son.

The disciples John and James were referred to as the "Sons of Thunder" because of their character.[8] Barnabas (which means "Son of Encouragement") was a name given to Joseph from Cyprus because of his encouraging nature.[9]

Don't get me wrong here; in calling God our Father, there's no way we're equal with Him. But it was in this profound Jewish context that Jesus told us to address God this way. Too often we don't take that concept far enough. We lose the meaning of it. We're offered an unspeakably high privilege by being invited to approach God in prayer as our Father.

Children

If God is our Father, then we're His children—sons and daughters of God. What a deal! Just as God has many titles, so do I. I'm a husband, father, and "gramper." I'm a minister, a worshiper, a teacher, and a pray-er. But my primary identity is none of these. My primary identity is that I'm a child of the heavenly Father!

Wonderful privileges come with this identity, as Romans 8:15–17[10]

---

8. **Mark 3:17,** James son of Zebedee and his brother John (to them he gave the name Boanerges, which means Sons of Thunder).

9. **Acts 4:36, Joseph,** a Levite from Cyprus, whom the apostles called Barnabas (which means Son of Encouragement).

10. **Romans 8:15–17,** For you did not receive a spirit that makes you a slave again to fear, but you received the Spirit of sonship. And by him we cry, "Abba, Father." The Spirit himself testifies with our spirit that we are God's children. Now if we are children, then

spells out: We have the privilege of approaching God boldly and calling Him *Abba* (Daddy!); we're His heirs—in line to inherit (with Christ) all He possesses[11]; and we get to walk in a newfound freedom.[12]

In 1 John 3:1, the old apostle can hardly contain himself when he thinks about this reality. Listen to him slowly as he speaks to us: "How great is the love the Father has lavished on us, that we should be called children of God! And that is what we are!" John saw that one of the ways the Father lavishes His love on us is that He does everything necessary for us to be called His children.

With this high calling there are also responsibilities. Because we're His dearly loved children, we're to imitate our Dad.[13] Romans 8:14[14] says we have a responsibility to follow Him. And in Matthew 5:43–48[15], Jesus says that because we're His children, we're to act completely differently from the way we normally

---

we are heirs—heirs of God and co-heirs with Christ, if indeed we share in his sufferings in order that we may also share in his glory.

11. **Galatians 4:6–7,** Because you are sons, God sent the Spirit of his Son into our hearts, the Spirit who calls out, "Abba, Father." So you are no longer a slave, but a son; and since you are a son, God has made you also an heir.

12. **Romans 8:21,** That the creation itself will be liberated from its bondage to decay and brought into the glorious freedom of the children of God.

13. **Ephesians 5:1,** Be imitators of God, therefore, as dearly loved children.

14. **Romans 8:14,** Because those who are led by the Spirit of God are sons of God.

15. **Matthew 5:43–48,** "You have heard that it was said, 'Love your neighbor and hate your enemy.' But I tell you: Love your enemies and pray for those who persecute you, that you may be sons of your Father in heaven. He causes his sun to rise on the evil and the good, and sends rain on the righteous and the unrighteous. If you love those who love you, what reward will you get? Are not even the tax collectors doing that? And if you greet only your brothers, what are you doing more than others? Do not even pagans do that? Be perfect, therefore, as your heavenly Father is perfect."

would, loving not just our neighbors but even our enemies! We're to pray for those who mistreat us and do good to those who don't do good to us. Why? Because that's how our Dad would do it! In fact, Jesus says, "Be perfect, therefore, as your heavenly Father is perfect" (Matthew 5:48). How's that possible? When we understand that the word for *perfect* here means "mature," we learn to ask the Spirit of God to let us act consistently with who we truly are. We really are His children. So we can say, "When I grow up, I want to be just like Daddy!"

Heavenly

This word *heavenly* refers not only to location but also to His character. It's not so much His address as it is His nature. Though He's our Father, He's not a buffed-up, polished-up version of our best example. As a friend of mine says, "He's not a bigger one of us!" The fact that we can call Him our Father doesn't bring Him down to our level. He's still the Most Holy One. He's still all-powerful. He's still worthy to be "feared above all gods".[16] He's still awesome. He's still the just Judge of the universe and all in it.

The word *heavenly* reminds us that although we get to come to Him and call Him our Father, we dare not become casual or seek to relate to Him as though He were somehow less than the Awesome Creator.

A beautiful balance is presented here. While *Father* speaks of the ways we can relate to Him, *heavenly* speaks of ways we cannot.

---

16. **1 Chronicles 16:25,** For great is the Lord and most worthy of praise; He is to be feared above all gods.

He's similar to us...yet different.

He's close to us...yet distant.

He's personal...yet infinite.

As we pray, we do well to maintain this balanced perspective.

Responding

1. Pray in the plural for a group you are part of, perhaps your family, your community, your congregation, your company, or your country.

2. What to you are the most significant privileges of being God's child? What to you are the most significant responsibilities? In prayer, talk to the Father about these.

3. Pray through some of the prayers from part 3 that relate to this line (17–23).

Chapter 5
"Let Your Name Be Holy..."
(On Earth As It Is in Heaven)

While I was in Birmingham, Alabama, to facilitate a Pastors' Prayer Summit, one early morning I found myself thinking and praying about how holiness refers to God's unique place in my life. My prayers repeated this pattern: "Jesus, You *alone* are..." And I filled in words and statements that describe His uniqueness.

During the first session of the summit later that morning, the Lord led us to read and pray from our favorite Jesus-exalting Scriptures. After a few minutes of wonderful prayer, one brother began singing a song about how "Christ alone" is our source of strength and hope. Another brother picked up on that and began to pray, "Jesus, You alone are my source of strength, You alone are my righteousness, You alone are the all-powerful One, You alone are the King of kings," and so on. This was exactly how I'd prayed earlier that morning. So I invited others to do the same.

For several minutes, Jesus received the praise of these pastors as many of us spoke out describing the uniqueness of Jesus. "Jesus, You alone are my Savior...the lover of my soul...the Alpha and Omega...the Creator and Sustainer of all things..." After several minutes of this, we sang the chorus: "You alone are my strength, my shield, to You alone may my spirit yield. You alone are my heart's desire, and I long to worship You." Then came more prayers beginning with "Jesus, You alone are..."

After a pause, someone began singing the hymn "Holy, Holy, Holy." Soon the room was filled with a sweet, majestic sense of the holiness of God. It was strong singing. We sang all four verses. As we concluded with "God in three Persons, blessed Trinity," we didn't want to stop. I sensed we should keep singing, making up our own melody but using only one word as lyrics—the word *Holy.* I gave a brief explanation and invited them to enter in. All forty-plus of us began to sing in wonderful melody and harmony, "Holy, holy, holy, holy…" Tenors harmonized above; basses filled in the bottom. We sang and sang. For six to eight minutes, there was a clear sense that we'd literally joined our worship with that of heaven, and the Holy Spirit was the director of our choir. We felt like we were singing with the seraphim in Isaiah 6 or the living creatures in Revelation 4.

While we were praising the Lord with our Jesus-You-alone-are prayers, we were proclaiming precisely what we were singing about: His *holiness.*

"Let Your name be holy" is the first of seven requests in this model prayer. Its position is significant. It may be the most important thing we pray. It may also be the most difficult to fully grasp.

Holy

Most of us have learned this line of the Lord's Prayer using the word *hallowed.* It sounds poetic, but we seldom use that word in English anymore, except maybe while describing hallways of old institutions.

Hallowed means "holy"—but what does *holy* mean? The short answer is that it means "set apart." It means to be different from everyone and everything else. Another word that may help us understand the meaning of *holy* is the word *sacred*. It is the same word Jesus uses in John 17:17 when He prays "Sanctify them by the truth."

Moses found himself standing on holy ground, so he was told to take his shoes off.[1] The Sabbath was holy, so on that day they were not to do things the way they did the rest of the week.[2] The priests were holy, so they were to act differently and be treated differently.[3] The tabernacle[4] and all its contents[5] were holy, so it was consecrated and different from all other tents.

The key thing about dealing with things that are holy or sacred is that we are to treat them *differently* from the way we treat those things that are not designated as holy.

And God Himself is holy. As the residents of heaven in both the Old Testament[6] and the New Testament[7] stood before God, the attribute they were most aware of was His holiness. They

---

1. **Exodus 3:5,** "Don't come any closer," God said. "Take off your sandals, for the place where you are standing is holy."

2. **Exodus 20:8,** "Remember the Sabbath day by keeping it holy."

3. **Exodus 29:1,** This is what you are to do to consecrate them, so they may serve me as priests...

4. **Exodus 26:33,** The curtain will separate the Holy Place from the Most Holy Place.

5. **Exodus 30:37,** Do not make any incense with this formula for yourselves; consider it holy to the Lord.

6. **Isaiah 6:2–3,** "Above him were seraphs, each with six wings: With two wings they covered their faces, with two they covered their feet, and with two they were flying. And they were calling to one another: 'Holy, holy, holy is the LORD Almighty; the whole earth is full of his glory.'"

7. **Revelation 4:8,** Each of the four living creatures had six wings and was covered with eyes all around, even under his wings. Day and night they never stop saying: "Holy, holy, holy is the Lord God Almighty, who was, and is, and is to come."

repeatedly cried out, "Holy, holy, holy," not because they couldn't think of anything else to say, but because that is the overwhelming characteristic of the One on the throne. He is holy, and we're not to treat Him and His name in the same manner we treat other people and names.

Sometimes we tend to think of holiness as "goodness on steroids"; someone who's really good is more "holy" than I am. Ultimate goodness is an important aspect of holiness, but holiness is far more than goodness. God is

Holiness is more about distinction than about perfection.

perfect, but holiness is more about distinction than about perfection. God isn't holy because He's good; He's good because He's holy. God didn't become incrementally better and better and therefore holier and holier. He is and always has been holy because He's completely set apart—entirely distinct from everything and everyone else. He's not like any of the rest of us. He's in a class all by Himself, completely unique.

This is the essence of what is meant when we say God is holy.

God asks, "Is there any God besides me? No, there is no other Rock. I know not one" (Isaiah 44:8). Now, when the One who is all-knowing says He doesn't know of any other god around, that's pretty significant. He longs for us to get this because "in the LORD alone are righteousness and strength" (Isaiah 45:24). He's the only source of righteousness, strength, and everything else we really need. And if that's the conclusion of the One who knows everything, it needs to be our conclusion as well.

So the specific request God wants us to pray first is that here on earth His Name would be seen and treated *differently* than everything else—just as it already is in heaven.

Name

God's name reflects His character. Though God has many titles, I have found only two actual names. I understand there are Scriptures that refer to God as having other names, [8] but I would suggest that these are obviously titles rather than actual names. So much of His character is reflected in His titles, but there are two specific aspects of His character that are reflected in His two names.

In the Old Testament, His name is *Yahweh* (or Jehovah), which in most English versions is translated as LORD (small caps). Very simply, this name means "I AM." This is what He said to Moses when Moses asked Him what His name was. [9]

In essence it tells us that *He is*—He is all He needs to be, at all times, in all places, in all situations. He is completely unique. How different that is from each of us!

In the New Testament, the Son's name is *Jesus*. This is the name the angel told Joseph to give to the baby growing inside Mary. [10]

---

8. Isaiah 7:14, Therefore the Lord himself will give you a sign: The virgin will be with child and will give birth to a son, and will call him Immanuel.

Isaiah 9:6, For to us a child is born, to us a son is given, and the government will be on his shoulders. And he will be called Wonderful Counselor, Mighty God, Everlasting Father, Prince of Peace.

9. Exodus 3:13–14, Moses said to God, "Suppose I go to the Israelites and say to them, 'The God of your fathers has sent me to you,' and they ask me, 'What is his name?' Then what shall I tell them?" God said to Moses, "I am who I am. This is what you are to say to the Israelites: 'I AM has sent me to you.'"

10. Matthew 1:21, She will give birth to a son, and you are to give him the name Jesus, because he will save his people from their sins.

In that same verse we find this name's meaning. His name is Jesus because He saves: "Because He will save his people from their sins!" The essence of the name and character of Jesus is that He's the Savior.

In my head, I summarize the meanings of these two names—"I AM" and "Savior"—with this little rhyming phrase: "I am there… and I care."

God is very concerned about the reputation and use of His name. Many times we see Him doing or saying things specifically because He wants His name to be seen as great, holy, or awesome. Consider the exodus,[11] military victories,[12] rescuing His people,[13] and the condition of His city and people.[14] Mary echoed the Psalmist[15] when she rejoiced at the news of her pregnancy and recognized the holiness of His name.[16]

---

11. **Exodus 6:7,** "I will take you as my own people, and I will be your God. Then you will know that I am the LORD your God, who brought you out from under the yoke of the Egyptians."

Exodus 9:16, "But I have raised you up for this very purpose, that I might show you my power and that my name might be proclaimed in all the earth."

12. **1 Kings 20:13, 28,** Meanwhile a prophet came to Ahab king of Israel and announced, "This is what the LORD says: 'Do you see this vast army? I will give it into your hand today, and then you will know that I am the LORD.' The man of God came up and told the king of Israel, "This is what the LORD says: 'Because the Arameans think the LORD is a god of the hills and not a god of the valleys, I will deliver this vast army into your hands, and you will know that I am the LORD.'"

Ezekiel 39:6, "I will send fire on Magog and on those who live in safety in the coastlands, and they will know that I am the LORD."

13. **Isaiah 43:3, 11, 15,** For I am the LORD, your God, the Holy One of Israel, your Savior; I give Egypt for your ransom, Cush and Seba in your stead.… I, even I, am the LORD, and apart from me there is no savior… I am the LORD, your Holy One, Israel's Creator, your King.

Joel 3:17, "Then you will know that I, the LORD your God, dwell in Zion, my holy hill. Jerusalem will be holy; never again will foreigners invade her."

14. **Daniel 9:19** O Lord, listen! O Lord, forgive! O Lord, hear and act! For your sake, O my God, do not delay, because your city and your people bear your Name.

15. **Psalm 111:9,** He provided redemption for his people; he ordained his covenant forever—holy and awesome is his name.

16. **Luke 1:49,** For the Mighty One has done great things for me—holy is his name.

And the third of the Ten Commandments states very clearly never to misuse His name.[17]

God's holiness relates to His two names in that He's uniquely qualified to fulfill the meaning of both of them. He's the *only One* who's really there everywhere and all the time and the *only One* who really does care fully and completely. I'm grateful that there are people who are there for us on many occasions and who show their care for us in many ways. But this in no way compares to the wonderful presence and care that comes from our ever-present and all-caring God. He's the only One who can say and actually mean, "I will never leave you."[18] He's the only One who knows every specific way in which we need personal care. He's the only One who not only *knows* the answer to our deepest needs, but actually *is* the answer.

Praise or Request?

We often view this line as a statement of worship or adoration. Believe me, I'm all for worshiping and adoring our wonderful Lord; we should be fanatical worshipers. But is this line really an invitation or instruction to worship and adore Him—a call to praise Him?

Actually, it is the first request of this prayer. This is a request to *let* His name be holy—which takes place as we look to Him and allow Him to have a unique (holy) place in our lives.

So how do we do that? How do we let His name be holy here on earth as it is in heaven?

Sometimes we gain understanding of a concept by looking at its opposite. The opposite of making God's name holy is to make

---

17. **Exodus 20:7 and Deuteronomy 5:11,** You shall not misuse the name of the LORD your God, for the LORD will not hold anyone guiltless who misuses his name.

18. **Hebrews 13:5b,** "Never will I leave you. Never will I forsake you."

it profane or common. Unholiness describes something that is not simply bad, but something that is the *same* as everything else around it.

Profanity is a very serious sin. It's a violation of one of God's "top ten." It's using God's holy name without grasping its real meaning; we're regarding it only as "common" or "profane."

Profanity has to do with our words, but also with much more. In graphic language, Ezekiel 36:16–23[19] describes how God's people made His great name "profane." They did it not by "swearing" or by using His name mindlessly, which is what we might typically think. Rather, it was by the way God's people *acted.* The people of Israel belonged to the Lord, but their actions weren't consistent with that. They acted as badly as or even worse than those who didn't claim to be God's followers. They acted as though God wasn't real.

In the conclusion of this passage, God restated for them His intention by saying, "'Then the nations will know that I am the Lord,' declares the Sovereign Lord, 'when I show myself holy through you before their eyes.'" Don't miss those words *through you.* God's desire is that *we* would be channels through which His name is seen as holy here on earth. God has chosen to let His character (His name) be known and shown to those around us by the way we represent Him.

---

19. **Ezekiel 36:16–23,** Again the word of the Lord came to me: "Son of man, when the people of Israel were living in their own land, they defiled it by their conduct and their actions. Their conduct was like a woman's monthly uncleanness in my sight. So I poured out my wrath on them because they had shed blood in the land and because they had defiled it with their idols. I dispersed them among the nations, and they were scattered through the countries; I judged them according to their conduct and their actions. And wherever they went among the nations they profaned my holy name, for it was said of them, 'These are the Lord's people, and yet they had to leave his land.' I had concern for my holy name, which the house of Israel profaned among the nations where they had gone. "Therefore say to the house of Israel, This is what the Sovereign Lord says: It is not for your sake, O house of Israel, that I am going to do these things, but for the sake of my holy name, which you have profaned among the nations where you have gone. I will show the holiness of my great name, which has been profaned among the nations, the name you have profaned among them. Then the nations will know that I am the Lord, declares the Sovereign Lord, when I show myself holy through you before their eyes.'"

We let God's name be holy (unique) here on earth as it is in heaven by treating it differently than we treat any other name. We do it by treating Him differently than any other person. We do it by acting as though He really is with us in all situations (He is "I AM") and really does care about us (He is "The Savior"). Whenever we depend on someone or something else to be our "I AM" or our Savior, we make His name common and unholy.

But before His name can be holy *through* us, it must first be holy *to* us. We must be fully convinced, in our heads and in our hearts, that He really is both our I AM and our Savior. Then His name will be holy *through* us to others all around, and the result will be more of heaven here on earth.

Our prayer can be that in every situation throughout the day, our actions would demonstrate and communicate this message from Him: "I am there, and I care." As we pray and live this way, people around us will know we really do belong to a God whose name is holy.

———

Responding

1. *Take time to adore Christ by praying some "Jesus, You alone are" prayers as described in the beginning of this chapter.*

2. *What is one way you can be more consistent in treating God and His name more holy? Ask Him to help you make His name holy in your life in those specific areas.*

3. *Pray through some of the prayers from part 3 that relate to this line (24–28).*

Chapter 6
"Let Your Kingdom Come..."
(On Earth As It Is in Heaven)

I remember an afternoon I once spent within sight of Mount Ararat in eastern Turkey. I was leading a small group traveling through Turkey and praying for God's work to be more released in this nation. We talked to a few people who knew English and spent much time in prayer.

We chose to have lunch that afternoon in a small restaurant where we recognized the word *Pizza* painted on the window. Inside, the first thing I noticed was the corner-mounted television playing a dubbed rerun of an American soap opera. The words were Turkish, but the plot was definitely American. And on my can of Pepsi, which I ordered with the pizza, was an advertisement about an upcoming Michael Jackson concert in Istanbul. I grieved at what we had exported to this nation.

After finishing the pizza, we drove to a rather secluded field. We felt led of the Lord to spread out over this field and pray. The two American culture "gifts" I'd observed in the restaurant were a great contrast to why we'd come to this country. They caused me to repent for what our country had given Turkey and gave me a great motivation to pray for God's kingdom to come to this nation.

My prayers on this occasion were intense. I cried out to the Lord to bring His kingdom values rather than our culture to the dear people we'd met. I prayed that His righteousness, peace, and joy would pervade this nation and culture, that Jesus would be exalted as King in their lives.

Several months later, I was reading a newsletter from the "Friends of Turkey" ministry. The ministry's director commented that they were seeing new freedom and fruit in Turkey. He said there was more openness to receiving and reading Bibles, watching the *Jesus* video, and being converted to Christ in the past several months than he'd ever seen in his twenty years of ministry there.

I knew the group I'd been with were not the only ones praying for this country, but I was excited, humbled, and grateful that our prayers had made a kingdom difference.

To pray for the Lord's kingdom to come means to surrender to the rulership of Jesus Christ. We're inviting Him to come and be King in and through our lives.

How can we tell the difference between His kingdom and ours? Asking some simple questions can help: What's my focus? How do I use my influence and my resources? What's my passion and concern? What are the motives behind my actions? Whose reputation am I concerned about? Whose opinion and desires matter most to me? Whose standards am I seeking to uphold? Whose future is most important to me? Whose words (or Word) influence me most?

Can we honestly say that His kingdom is more important to us than ours?

What His Kingdom Is Like

Before we look at the kingdom of God, think with me about kingdoms in general. What is necessary before you can have an earthly kingdom? At least four things: *a king, subjects, territory,* and *laws.* God's kingdom needs the same things. Obviously, Jesus is the King. Hallelujah! We are the subjects. Where we go is the territory. And His kingdom principles are laid out in His Word.

So the kingdom we're praying for can be defined in brief as the realm over which Jesus is ruling as King. That kingdom is both "here and now" and "there and then." It's both now and not yet. It will be ultimately fulfilled in the future,[1] but those who have been redeemed get to live in His kingdom right now.[2] This is seen in Paul's prayer for the Colossians, when he says our rescue from the domain of darkness has "brought us into the kingdom of the Son He loves" (Colossians 1:13).

Jesus was always looking for ways to explain His kingdom to His disciples. Matthew's Gospel devotes an entire chapter to His parables about the kingdom. Perhaps He was remembering how Martha made bread when He said, for example, that the kingdom was like yeast that a woman kneaded into flour, till all of it was leavened (13:33); God's kingdom permeates everything it touches. Or He noticed another opportunity when He saw

---

1. Revelation 11:15, The seventh angel sounded his trumpet, and there were loud voices in heaven, which said: "The kingdom of the world has become the kingdom of our Lord and of his Christ, and he will reign for ever and ever."

Revelation 19:6, Then I heard what sounded like a great multitude, like the roar of rushing waters and like loud peals of thunder, shouting: "Hallelujah! For our Lord God Almighty reigns."

2. Luke 17:21, Nor will people say, 'Here it is,' or 'There it is,' because the kingdom of God is within you."

some seeds in the market. He said the kingdom is like the tiny mustard seed that grows into a tree; God's kingdom may be small right now, but one day it will be huge (13:31).

In His many parables in Matthew 13, Jesus taught that His kingdom is communicated through words;[3] it must be received to be effective;[4] it has a real enemy;[5] it contains both wheat and weeds;[6] it starts small, like a mustard seed,[7] and it infiltrates like yeast.[8] His kingdom is of great value,[9] and it also values us greatly.[10] And His kingdom is a kingdom of separation.[11] Each of these truths can be turned into meaningful prayers.

---

3. **Matthew 13:19,** "When anyone hears the message about the kingdom and does not understand it, the evil one comes and snatches away what was sown in his heart. This is the seed sown along the path."

4. **Matthew 13:22,** "The one who received the seed that fell among the thorns is the man who hears the word, but the worries of this life and the deceitfulness of wealth choke it, making it unfruitful."

5. **Matthew 13:25,**"But while everyone was sleeping, his enemy came and sowed weeds among the wheat, and went away."

6. **Matthew 13:29–30,** "'No,' he answered, 'because while you are pulling the weeds, you may root up the wheat with them. Let both grow together until the harvest. At that time I will tell the harvesters: First collect the weeds and tie them in bundles to be burned; then gather the wheat and bring it into my barn.'"

7. **Matthew 13: 31,** He told them another parable: "The kingdom of heaven is like a mustard seed, which a man took and planted in his field."

8. **Matthew 13: 33,** He told them still another parable: "The kingdom of heaven is like yeast that a woman took and mixed into a large amount of flour until it worked all through the dough."

9. **Matthew 13: 44,** "The kingdom of heaven is like treasure hidden in a field. When a man found it, he hid it again, and then in his joy went and sold all he had and bought that field."

10. **Matthew 13: 45,** "Again, the kingdom of heaven is like a merchant looking for fine pearls."

11. **Matthew 13: 49,** "This is how it will be at the end of the age. The angels will come and separate the wicked from the righteous."

Another kingdom parable is found in Mark 4:26–29[12]. This one is about the mysterious way that scattered seed grows into ripened grain ready for harvest. We learn from this that the kingdom must be planted before it grows. Its growth is continuous and isn't ultimately dependent on our own labors or limited to our understanding. In fact, we may not be able to understand it at all! The kingdom grows "all by itself," in a prescribed progression. And it must be harvested at the right time to yield that for which it was intended. These too are things we can incorporate into our prayers for His kingdom.

The one verse I've found most helpful in praying for the kingdom is Romans 14:17: "For the kingdom of God is not a matter of eating and drinking, but of righteousness, peace and joy in the Holy Spirit." In my times of personal prayer, this verse has opened up more vistas and possibilities than any other kingdom passage. I've prayed it many times for myself, my family, congregations, ministries, and communities. I encourage you to let the Lord use this verse to expand your praying for God's kingdom.

This clear statement made by the Holy Spirit through Paul tells us what that kingdom is made of—righteousness, peace, and joy in the Holy Spirit—and how it's built. It helps us recognize His kingdom in us, in those around us, and in our world.

---

12. **Mark 4:26–29,** He also said, "This is what the kingdom of God is like. A man scatters seed on the ground. Night and day, whether he sleeps or gets up, the seed sprouts and grows, though he does not know how. All by itself the soil produces grain—first the stalk, then the head, then the full kernel in the head. As soon as the grain is ripe, he puts the sickle to it, because the harvest has come."

Righteousness is simply right standing with God and with those around me. With God, our righteousness comes not because we "do it right" all the time, but because we've said yes to the work of Jesus on the cross.[13] With others, our righteousness comes from saying yes to the way He has designed relationships to work. We let His priorities determine our relational responsibilities. Praying for God's kingdom includes praying that His righteousness will shape my relationships.

Peace is a natural result of righteousness. Romans 5:1 says that since I'm justified (declared righteous by God), I have peace with God. This peace is designed to spill over and affect all my other relationships. It's one of the evidences that the Spirit of God is at work in us.[14] It's something we can help establish as peacemakers[15] and give to others. God says we can acquire peace in two specific ways: through loving His law, which is His Word[16] and by keeping our minds on Him.[17] Philippians 4:6–9[18]

13. **2 Corinthians 5:21,** God made him who had no sin to be sin for us, so that in him we might become the righteousness of God.

14. **Galatians 5:22–23,** But the fruit of the Spirit is love, joy, peace, patience, kindness, goodness, faithfulness, gentleness and self-control. Against such things there is no law.

15. **Matthew 5:9,** "Blessed are the peacemakers. For they will be called the sons of God."

16. **Psalm 119:165,** Great peace have they who love your law, and nothing can make them stumble.

17. **Isaiah 26:3,** You will keep in perfect peace him whose mind is steadfast, because he trusts in you.

18. **Philippians 4:6–9,** Do not be anxious about anything, but in everything, by prayer and petition, with thanksgiving, present your requests to God. And the peace of God, which transcends all understanding, will guard your hearts and your minds in Christ Jesus. Finally, brothers, whatever is true, whatever is noble, whatever is right, whatever is pure, whatever is lovely, whatever is admirable—if anything is excellent or praiseworthy—think about such things. Whatever you have learned or received or heard from me, or seen in me—put it into practice. And the God of peace will be with you.

tells us that both the peace of God and the God of peace will be active in our lives if we respond to life situations with prayer and proper perspective.

The *joy* that's characteristic of His kingdom isn't just any old joy, but Holy Spirit joy! It comes from that deep, abiding confidence that God is at work no matter what our situation. While happiness is dependent on what happens, joy depends on the God who makes things happen. It's the anticipation of receiving that which I greatly desire. Knowing that God is able to use any situation we face to make us more like Him[19] gives us an unstoppable supply of Holy Spirit joy. And that joy gives us strength to keep on keeping on.[20]

When we pray that God's kingdom of righteousness, peace, and joy in the Holy Spirit will continue to increase in us and through us, the answers will be obvious. We'll see godly relationships in homes, in congregations, and in neighborhoods. We'll see real peace and joy displayed between family members, neighbors, co-workers, and leaders. We'll see businesspeople making decisions based on how it will affect the reputation of their King. We'll see teachers and counselors helping students value one another as more important than themselves. We'll see Christians who've been

---

19. **Romans 8:28–29,** And we know that in all things God works for the good of those who love him, who have been called according to his purpose. For those God foreknew he also predestined to be conformed to the likeness of his Son, that he might be the firstborn among many brothers.

20. **Nehemiah 8:10,** Nehemiah said, "Go and enjoy choice food and sweet drinks, and send some to those who have nothing prepared. This day is sacred to our Lord. Do not grieve, for the joy of the LORD is your strength."

offended by another believer humble themselves and reestablish their relationship. All this is the kingdom displayed. This is the kingdom of God at work.

How His Kingdom Comes

Sometimes I've caught myself using this part of the prayer like a shotgun while hunting quail. "There...right *there*...that's where the kingdom of God needs to be." I load the chamber, raise the barrel, take careful aim, and pull the trigger, expecting to see more of His kingdom in the situation I have in my sights. But the more I pray this, the more I'm convinced that the way He wants to get His kingdom from heaven to earth is *through you*

We are to be kingdom carriers. *and me.* When we see situations that need more of His kingdom, we're to go there and bring the kingdom with us. Then more of His kingdom is there. We are to be kingdom carriers.

That's how Jesus did it. He knew there needed to be more of the kingdom of God on earth, so He came here and brought the kingdom with Him.

We don't know all the specifics of how His kingdom comes in and through us. But Scripture shows us several ways, and knowing these can help generate many effective kingdom prayers.

First, the kingdom comes through our repentance. As their ministries began, both Jesus and John the Baptist proclaimed, "Repent, for the kingdom of heaven is near" (Matthew 3:2; 4:17). As we repent, let's remember to be like the believers at Thessalonica: They turned *to* something, not just away from something.[21] Our first step in receiving more of His kingdom life is to repent *to* His kingdom and *away from* everything that's not under His rulership.

Second, it comes to those who are "poor in spirit" (Matthew 5:3). This is another way of saying we recognize that we have no spiritual currency to buy any spiritual goods. We can't pull out cash or plastic, plunk it down on the counter, and expect spiritual growth in return. Kingdom growth comes to those who recognize they don't have what it takes, in and of themselves, to grow in His kingdom. We're dependent on Him in everything.[22]

The third way His kingdom comes in us and through us is by our praise. Psalm 22:3 tells us that the Lord is enthroned on the praises of Israel. When we, His subjects, give praise to the King, more of His reign is established.

Whether we are in good times or bad, easy times or hard, when we turn our hearts and minds toward Him, responding to His Word and recognizing His worth, His kingdom comes. Sometimes the situation changes, as when Paul and Silas were in prison (Acts 16:22–30), and an instant release takes place. Sometimes the situation doesn't change, as when Shadrach, Meshach, and Abednego were in the furnace (Daniel 3:8–30) or as when Daniel was in the lion's den (6:1–28), and God brings glory to His name (and promotion to His people) through protecting

---

21. **1 Thessalonians 1:9–10,** For they themselves report what kind of reception you gave us. They tell how you turned to God from idols to serve the living and true God, and to wait for his Son from heaven, whom he raised from the dead—Jesus, who rescues us from the coming wrath.

22. **John 15:5b,** "Apart from me you can do nothing."

us in the midst of the situation. But the King (and the kingdom) always comes at the sound of our praise.[23]

A fourth way is found in the words of Paul and Barnabas in Acts 14:22. Paul had just been beaten and left for dead. Miraculously, he picked himself up, went with Barnabas back to the cities they'd just left, and began "strengthening the disciples and encouraging them to remain true to the faith." Their message: "We must go through many hardships to enter the kingdom of God." We're so far away from the kingdom standard that it often takes the anvil of hardships to help us get pounded back into our original design. If this method was good enough for Jesus,[24] Paul, and other New Testament disciples, it should be good enough for us as well.

Finally, His kingdom comes as we pursue it. Jesus gives His best things not to the casual inquirer, but to those who seek Him with all their heart.[25] Jesus tells us to "seek first his kingdom and his righteousness" (Matthew 6:33); then we'll experience not only His wonderful rulership over our lives, but all the other things we really need as well.

One of Jesus' parables compares the kingdom to a man who found a buried treasure in someone's field,[26] and became totally committed to getting it. The kingdom of God is so valuable that the only sane thing to do is pursue it wholeheartedly, with everything we have.

---

23. **James 4:8,** Come near to God and he will come near to you.

24. **Hebrews 5:8,** Although he was a son, he learned obedience from what he suffered.

25. **Jeremiah 29:13,** "You will seek me and find me when you seek me with all your heart."

26. **Matthew 13:44,** "The kingdom of heaven is like treasure hidden in a field. When a man found it, he hid it again, and then in his joy went and sold all he had and bought that field."

When we pray to have His kingdom come, we are not only praying for a very good and real future event, we're praying that He'll allow us to see His kingdom and pursue it today. We're telling Him we want Him to use whatever methods, circumstances, or people necessary to develop in us His righteousness, His peace, and His joy—right here and right now.

Responding

1. Which truth about the kingdom of God mentioned in this chapter brings the greatest excitement and anticipation to you? Pray that that trait of His kingdom would dominate every area of your life.

2. Pray through the five ways God's kingdom comes, and tell the Lord you are willing to cooperate with Him in these processes.

3. Pray through some of the prayers from part 3 that relate to this line (29–35).

Chapter 7
"Let Your Will Be Done..."
(On Earth As It Is in Heaven)

One morning as I was praying, I had a very clear thought from the Lord I never remembered thinking or hearing before. It was as if I heard Him say, "My commands are the best expression of My will." Understanding this truth has changed the way I pray and live. It has allowed me to pray with far greater confidence.

I had the opportunity to work with the Luis Palau team in preparing for their 2008 citywide evangelistic festival in Portland, Oregon. During a team meeting, I was asked to lead us in a time of prayer. I simply invited them to "pray only those things that you know to be God's will." We prayed very large prayers. We prayed that Jesus' name would be lifted high over the city, that the church would be drawn together in unity, that many people would come to know and love the Savior in the coming months, and that real needs of widows and orphans and the poor would be met. No one added the phrase "If it be Your will" to their requests because we were praying around His clear commands. This allowed us to pray great prayers with great confidence.

When we read God's commands that we submit to one another,[1] pray for our leaders,[2] pray for our city,[3] speak up

---

1. **Ephisians 5:21,** Submit to one another out of reverence for Christ.

2. **1 Timothy 2:1–2,** I urge, then, first of all, that requests, prayers, intercession and thanksgiving be made for everyone—for kings and all those in authority, that we may live peaceful and quiet lives in all godliness and holiness.

3. **Jeremiah 29:7,** Also, seek the peace and prosperity of the city to which I have carried you into exile. Pray to the LORD for it, because if it prospers, you too will prosper.

for those who can't speak for themselves,[4] do the work of an evangelist,[5] or disciple others,[6] we do not need to wonder if this is God's will for us. <u>If He tells us to do it, we can know it is His will.</u>

If His will is expressed in His commands, it follows that the *greatest* expression of His will is reflected in His *greatest* commandments. Jesus states what those are:

"'Love the Lord your God with all your heart and with all your soul and with all your mind and with all your strength.' The second is this: 'Love your neighbor as yourself.' There is no commandment greater than these." (Mark 12:30–31)

From this it's clear that the greatest fulfillment of His will happens when we love Him and love others. Every time we act in love, we're accomplishing His will. Every time we don't, we aren't.

This makes it especially important to have a good understanding of what this word *love* means. Since God wants us to grasp this concept (His love for us, our love for Him, and our love for others) more than any other, it seems to be a primary target for the evil one. He has convinced our culture that love is either a physical, sexual act or a nice warm emotion. It is something we either fall into or out of. But God's love, the

---

4. **Proverbs 31:8–9,** Speak up for those who cannot speak for themselves, for the rights of all who are destitute. Speak up and judge fairly; defend the rights of the poor and needy.

5. **2 Timothy 4:5,** But you, keep your head in all situations, endure hardship, do the work of an evangelist, discharge all the duties of your ministry.

6. **Matthew 28:18–20,** Then Jesus came to them and said, "All authority in heaven and on earth has been given to me. Therefore go and make disciples of all nations, baptizing them in the name of the Father and of the Son and of the Holy Spirit, and teaching them to obey everything I have commanded you. And surely I am with you always, to the very end of the age."

kind of love He demonstrates to us[7] and calls us to is something significantly different! Our love for others can be expressed and recognized through warm emotions or physical intimacy, but that is the caboose, not the engine.

From a biblical perspective, this love toward others means freely giving of myself for the highest good of another, desiring but not requiring a closer relationship with them. This understanding helps us as we pray for God's will to be done. It focuses our prayers toward specific kinds of actions.

Knowing that His greatest command (and therefore the greatest expression of His will) is that we love Him and others, our greatest prayers are that, by His grace, He would allow us to deepen our love relationship with Him and with those around us. This is both the greatest prayer request and the greatest answer to prayer. It's right that we pray it fervently and frequently.

> **Our greatest prayers are that, by His grace, He would allow us to deepen our love relationship with Him and with those around us.**

I want to give you a few other simple statements about God's will that can help us pray with more confidence.

God's Will Is Better than Ours

This may seem way too obvious, but I believe we all need to fully embrace this statement and live consistently with it.

Consider how this worked out in Jesus' life. He knew He

---

7. **Romans 5:8,** But God demonstrates his own love for us in this: While we were still sinners, Christ died for us.

was entering the world to do His Father's will.[8] Yet at the end of His earthly life, in Gethsemane, He faced the most critical decision of His ministry. With "loud cries and tears", He needed to freshly embrace the will of the Father over His own. Knowing fully what the cross meant, He "fell with his face to the ground and prayed, 'My Father, if it is possible, may this cup be taken from me. Yet not as I will, but as you will'" (Matthew 26:39).

Mary, His mother, also demonstrated her conviction that God's will was better than her own. It happened after the angel had told her the amazing news that she, a virgin, would be the mother of the Messiah. Understandably, she recognized how this would bring real difficulty into her life. Yet she simply responded, "May it be to me as you have said" (Luke 1:38).

I've made the best and most important decisions of my life when I've said the same thing. Initially, this happened when I consciously determined that by His grace I would live according to His will, not mine. That decision came years ago, when I was a summer camp counselor. I'd memorized Romans 12:1–2, and late on a Thursday night, as I lay on my bed in the darkness, I considered the implications of this passage for my life. I considered the rich mercies of God I'd received all my life and how selfishly I'd responded to them. I was so convicted by the contrast of His mercy and my self-centeredness that I surrendered all I knew of my

---

8. **Hebrews 10:5–7,** Therefore, when Christ came into the world, he said: "Sacrifice and offering you did not desire, but a body you prepared for me; with burnt offerings and sin offerings you were not pleased. Then I said, 'Here I am—it is written about me in the scroll—I have come to do your will, O God.'"

life to His will. That was the most significant decision of my life. But time and again I need to reapply it to other decisions I face on a daily basis.

At Present, His Will Isn't Always Accomplished on Earth

Otherwise, why would Jesus have told us to pray in this way?

As an example of this, we know that God really does want all people to be saved. He's "not wanting anyone to perish, but everyone to come to repentance" (2 Peter 3:9); He "wants all men to be saved and to come to a knowledge of the truth" (1 Timothy 2:4). But the truth is that not all people have been or will be saved.

Scripture seems to be pretty clear on this. There are things on earth the Father really wants to see happen that haven't happened, are not happening now, and won't happen later. In this regard, it's helpful to understand His will more as His desires rather than as a series of decrees He has made.

His Will Can Be Known and Done

This is clear from Paul's words to us in Ephesians 5. He encourages us to "find out what pleases the Lord" (v. 10) and to "understand what the Lord's will is" (v. 17). Likewise, Paul's prayer for the Colossian Christians was for "God to fill you with the knowledge of His will" (Colossians 1:9).

By depending on Him, it's possible not only to know His will but to do it. This assumption is clear in several passages.[9]

---

9. Matthew 7:21, "Not everyone who says to me, 'Lord, Lord,' will enter the kingdom of heaven, but only he who does the will of my Father who is in heaven."

John 14:15, "If you love me, you will obey what I command."

Our coming to know His will is for one purpose only—*doing* it.

Christians Want to Know and Do His Will

While I was pastoring a church, it wasn't uncommon for new followers of Jesus to come to me asking about God's will. This was always encouraging to me because I saw it as a sign that they were really wanting to follow Jesus. Those who don't care about that aren't very concerned about knowing His will. It's those who want to keep in step with His Spirit[10] who are eager to learn His will.

Paul demonstrated this desire from the start. On the road to Damascus, he asked the resurrected Lord, "What shall I do, Lord?" (Acts 22:10). And later he was able to say, "I was not disobedient to the heavenly vision" (26:19). He wanted to know and do God's will.

His Will Is Clearly Laid Out for Us in Scripture

Much (if not most) of God's will is clearly laid out in His Word. We tend to think that the greatest questions regarding His will are about various decisions like which person to marry, which job to take, which car to buy. But I've seen that His will is less about what we do and more about who we *are* and *why* we do what we do. There certainly are specific actions He wants us to take or not take, but there's more stated about inward traits He wants us to develop (such

---

Hebrews 10:36, You need to persevere so that when you have done the will of God, you will receive what he has promised.

1 John 2:17, The world and its desires pass away, but the man who does the will of God lives forever.

10. **Galatians 5:25,** Since we live by the Spirit, let us keep in step with the Spirit.

as the beatitudes in Matthew 5 or the fruit of the Spirit in Galatians 5) than about outward specifics of our behavior.

So whenever we pray consistently with Scripture—such as, "Lord, help me be filled with Your Spirit today" (Ephesians 5:18), or, "Father, today I recognize that apart from You, I can do nothing" (John 15:5)—we're praying according to His will.

His will is less about what we do and more about who we *are* and *why* we do what we do.

Some things in Scripture are specifically labeled as being God's will, as in these passages: "*It is God's will* that you should be sanctified; that you should avoid sexual immorality" (1 Thessalonians 4:3). "Be joyful always; pray continually; give thanks in all circumstances, for *this is God's will for you* in Christ Jesus" (5:16–18). "For *it is God's will* that by doing good you should silence the ignorant talk of foolish men" (1 Peter 2:15). We don't have to pray for guidance on whether to do these things. All we have to do is apply the grace to obey these statements.

Praying for God's will to be done doesn't mean using "if it's Your will" as a blanket phrase to cover all our requests. Sort of like, "God, please erase any part of this prayer I shouldn't have prayed!" I believe God wants us to understand what His will is (Ephesians 5:10, 17) so we can pray specifically in that direction. So with Micah 6:8 and Philippians 2:4 in mind, for example, we can tell Him, "Father, since it's clearly Your will that I walk in humility before You and others, give me opportunities to consider others more important than myself, and help me prefer their desires over my own." We can pray this with confidence and fully expect it to be answered.

Because the apostle John wanted us to understand this truth, he wrote, "This is the confidence we have in approaching God: that if we ask anything according to his will, he hears us. And if we know that he hears us—whatever we ask—we know that we have what we asked of him? (1 John 5:14–15)

Finally, notice the deep riches and encouragement of the following prayer—centered on God's will—found in Hebrews 13:20–21.

May the God of peace, who through the blood of the eternal covenant brought back from the dead our Lord Jesus, that great Shepherd of the sheep, equip you with everything good *for doing His will,* and may He work in us what is pleasing to Him, through Jesus Christ, to whom be glory for ever and ever. Amen.

Responding

1. Pray several prayers that you know without a doubt to be God's will.

2. Pray that you and one other person you care about would fulfill the two great commandments better. Pray that you will increase in your love for the Lord and other people.

3. Pray through some of the prayers from part 3 that relate to this line (36–38).

A Final Word About These First Three Requests

Jesus has given us a tremendous gift in telling us these three requests. They reflect the heart of the Father. I would encourage you to spend much time meditating on these three lines. As you do, He will show you more and more about His character and His desire for all people. I offer you one more way as a summary of how to pray this first part of the prayer.

Just as we are to pray that each of these three divine requests would happen here on earth as they are happening in heaven, so also we should pray that these three things are accomplished in us so they can be accomplished through us. Specifically, I would encourage you to pray that…

- His name would be holy *to* you so that it will be holy *through* you;
- His kingdom would come *in* you so that it will come *through* you;
- His will would be done *by* you so that it will be done *through* you.

To, in, and *by*—these three small prepositions capture three large propositions!

Chapter 8
"Give Us Today Our Daily Bread..."

Some of my best memories from early childhood are of smelling and eating Aunt Hannah's bread. She cooked on an old-fashioned wood-fueled stove—perhaps that was her secret. She raised six kids and baked about that many loaves of bread each week. Coming into her tiny house as she was taking the bread out of the oven and putting it on the bread racks meant we had to be patient only a few more minutes before we could cut into it, spread a large quantity of butter and perhaps some fresh berry jam on it, and savor the experience.

"Give us today our daily bread" is a line I've prayed for many years. One day, in the spring of 2000, the aroma of this line became much stronger for me than it had ever been before. It culminated in these words:

Give us this day our daily bread

Feed us, O Lord, or we'll not be fed

You are our life, You are our Lord

Feed us again from Your Living Word

Humbly we come, looking to You

Not just for bread but for all that we do

Feed us, O Lord, from Your gracious hand

Help us to hear Your daily commands

But more than the bread, more than anything else

What we need most is more of Yourself

Feed us, O Lord, from the Living One

Give us, O Lord, more of Your Son

This opening line in the second half of the Lord's Prayer can be easily overlooked. But if we do, we will miss some very valuable lessons. This line instructs us, humbles us, reminds us of what's really important, challenges us to a daily walk, and points us directly to the Savior.

This Day

Embracing this truth moves the entire prayer from historical appreciation to present application.

This line tells us first of all how often Jesus wants us to be praying this entire prayer: *daily*. It would be appropriate to add a *today* to the prayer's other lines: "Let Your will be done *today*," for example, or, "Forgive us *this day* as we forgive others." Embracing this truth moves the entire prayer from historical appreciation to present application. It tutors us to be aware of God's presence and activity as we move through each day.

This line also indicates what part of the day to pray this. If we're to ask Him for daily bread, He obviously wants us to ask before we eat it! Without any sense of legalism, I believe Jesus had in mind for us to pray through this prayer sometime early in the day—at least before we get hungry.

The emphasis on "today" in this line reminds us of two familiar Old Testament passages. In Joshua 24:15, Joshua challenges the people to "choose *this day* whom you will serve." Though given in a specific context, that challenge is a good reminder that on a daily basis we should be making that same choice to serve Him.

And in Psalm 118:24 we find the often-quoted verse, "*This is the day* the Lord has made; let us rejoice and be glad in it." Yes, each day is a special gift from the Lord to be celebrated. But notice the two prior verses in this psalm; this day the psalmist mentioned is when "the stone the builders rejected has become the capstone; the Lord has done this, and it is marvelous in our eyes" (vv. 22–23). It's the day when Jesus (the rejected stone) becomes the most important stone in the building—the day we celebrate the lordship of Jesus Christ.

So we can be reminded by two words in the prayer of our daily opportunity to surrender to Christ's lordship by choosing to follow Him fully throughout our day.

Give Us

The phrase *give us* tells us that when we come to Him, we're needy. We have needs we can't meet ourselves. As much as we'd like to think we're self-sufficient, we really are desperately dependent on God.

There's a story about a group of scientists who wanted to challenge God to a creation contest. With their increasing abilities to clone, they were feeling pretty confident about their chances. But as they scrapped some dirt together to begin their challenge, God told them, "Wait a minute. Get your own dirt! This is My dirt." It is His dirt. It's also His air, His water, His trees, His everything. So much for the "self-made" man.

Jesus said, "Apart from me you can do nothing" (John 15:5). Sometimes we may think that doesn't apply to our situation. But whatever we think we'll accomplish apart from Him really does end up being "nothing."

When it comes specifically to prayer, Paul says that "we don't even know what we should pray for, nor how we should pray" (Romans 8:26, NLT). We'll pray better when we understand how much we need His help even in the process! This is consistent with what Jesus says in Matthew 5:3: ("Blessed are the poor in spirit." Recognition of our own spiritual poverty is the starting point for effective prayer and deeper personal relationship with the Savior.) The best we have to offer God is simply our acknowledgment of our need of Him. Then He's free to work through us.

> **Recognition of our own spiritual poverty is the starting point for effective prayer and deeper personal relationship with the Savior.**

Note that Jesus doesn't invite us to come *buy* our daily bread. We have nothing anyway that would pay for it. The truth is, we're spiritually broke. There is no formula that will put us in a place where God is obligated to act in a certain way. Our only option is to come with nothing in our hands and simply ask. He wants us to come regularly with this understanding and ask Him for what we really need. When we do, our life and our prayers work better.

(This is especially necessary when we're doing things we've done many times before.) That's when we tend to think we're not nearly as dependent. I've preached countless times and have facilitated prayer in many different settings. So when I do those things again, (I need to be deliberate in recognizing my need for the Lord. My greatest danger on those occasions is to sense that I could do this without Him!)

This phrase, *give us*, reminds us that God is our only sufficient source. He's the only one qualified to meet our needs.

These words also tell us that He's not only able but willing to meet our needs. What would it be like to live in a world where God was able to meet our needs but was always grumpy, or stingy, or uncaring? But He invites us to come to Him and ask because He's compassionate and kind. He is *good.*

Our Daily Bread

Bread is a staple and a symbol of our need for food. It's also a symbol of every physical need we have. Jesus wants us to come to His Father regularly and ask Him to meet all our basic needs.

We should be careful before asking for too much beyond this, according to the advice of Agur in Proverbs 30:8–9. He asks that the Lord would give him "neither poverty nor riches, but *give me only my daily bread.* Otherwise, I may have too much and disown you and say 'Who is the LORD?' Or I may become poor and steal, and so dishonor the name of my God." Asking God for His balanced provision for us is part of the purpose of this prayer.

The phrase *daily bread* can also refer to our nonphysical needs. Though many Scriptures[1] indicate that our good Lord has

---

1. **Psalm 23:1,** The LORD is my shepherd; I shall not be in want.

    2 **Peter 1:3–4,** His divine power has given us everything we need for life and godliness through our knowledge of him who called us by his own glory and goodness. Through these he has given us his very great and precious promises, so that through them you may participate in the divine nature and escape the corruption in the world caused by evil desires.

    Ephesians 1:3, Praise be to the God and Father of our Lord Jesus Christ, who has blessed us in the heavenly realms with every spiritual blessing in Christ.

    1 **Corinthians 1:7,** Therefore you do not lack any spiritual gift as you eagerly wait for our Lord Jesus Christ to be revealed.

provided for us all that we need, it is still right that we present all our needs before Him in prayer.[2]

One of our greatest needs is for grace. God has invited us to come before His throne and ask for grace when we need it[3]— which is all the time. In our lives and relationships, grace is like oil to an engine, which won't run smoothly (or long) without it.

When others get the credit I think I deserve, I need grace. When others are invited and I'm not, I need grace. Scripture says God "gives grace to the humble" (James 4:6; 1 Peter 5:5). Every time I've intentionally humbled myself, I've felt a greater sense of His grace.

The "fruit of the Spirit" listed in Galatians 5:22–23 and the beatitudes of Matthew 5:3–10 are other examples of our non-physical needs. So is "wisdom that comes from heaven,"[4] which is available for the asking to those who lack it.[5]

All these things are loaves of the daily bread Jesus is baking in His oven, and He's willing to give it to us when we ask. Can you smell the aroma?

---

2. **Philippians 4:6–7,** Do not be anxious about anything, but in everything, by prayer and petition, with thanksgiving, present your requests to God. And the peace of God, which transcends all understanding, will guard your hearts and your minds in Christ Jesus.

3. **Hebrews 4:16,** Let us then approach the throne of grace with confidence, so that we may receive mercy and find grace to help us in our time of need.

4. **James 3:17,** But the wisdom that comes from heaven is first of all pure; then peace-loving, considerate, submissive, full of mercy and good fruit, impartial and sincere.

5. **James 1:5,** If any of you lacks wisdom, he should ask God, who gives generously to all without finding fault, and it will be given to him.

The bread can also represent God's provision, which requires our response. I have been told that this phrase has been used in nonbiblical writings to refer to military "rations." In biblical times, the captain was the one who recruited the troops to serve in his army.[6] The captain provided the goods, and the soldier followed the orders. In a very real sense, the orders were attached to the rations. If the recruit picked up the MREs (meals ready to eat), he was also committed to fulfilling the orders for that day. In a similar manner, as we pray in this way, we are recognizing that receiving God's provision is also our commitment to obey His orders for the day. "If we eat His bread, we do what He's said."

This daily bread also reminds us of the daily truth God wants to give us from His Word. Deuteronomy 8:3[7] and Matthew 4:4[8] tell us that God wants us to be living by "every word that proceeds out of the mouth of God." The manna God gave to the Israelites was to remind them of their continuous (daily) need for what God had to say to them. Each day, God has fresh-baked bread for us.

The first responsibility of the priest of the Old Testament[9]

---

6. **2 Timothy 2:4,** No one serving as a soldier gets involved in civilian affairs—he wants to please his commanding officer.

7. **Deuteronomy 8:3,** He humbled you, causing you to hunger and then feeding you with manna, which neither you nor your fathers had known, to teach you that man does not live on bread alone but on every word that comes from the mouth of the LORD.

8. **Matthew 4:4,** Jesus answered, "It is written: 'Man does not live on bread alone, but on every word that comes from the mouth of God.'"

9. **Leviticus 6:12,** The fire on the altar must be kept burning; it must not go out. Every morning the priest is to add firewood and arrange the burnt offering on the fire and burn the fat of the fellowship offerings on it.

was to keep the fire burning by putting another log on. We keep the fire of our devotion to Christ alive by putting another "log" from His Word onto our life each day. The pattern of Adam and Eve was, evidently, a daily walk with the Lord in the evening.[10] There's a blessing for those who listen to Him, "watching daily" at His doors[11] like a servant always ready to hear and do the master's bidding.

As we pray for daily manna, we're asking God to give us the truth we need for the situations we'll be facing—both for ourselves and for those around us. We need His daily perspectives to live righteous lives in the midst of an unrighteous world. And as we ask Him, He delights to give us just what we need. Many times as I've prepared to preach a sermon, a spiritual truth I just "happened to come across" in my personal time in the Word, from a passage seemingly unrelated to the text I was working on, became a key part of the message. Many times a truth I saw in my personal time in His Word became exactly what was needed by someone I had contact with later in the day. Because I got the bread in the morning, I was able to share it with others throughout the day.

---

10. **Genesis 3:8,** Then the man and his wife heard the sound of the LORD God as he was walking in the garden in the cool of the day, and they hid from the LORD God among the trees of the garden.

11. **Proverbs 8:34,** Blessed is the man who listens to me, watching daily at my doors, waiting at my doorway.

Bread of Life

The ultimate question about this daily bread is not what it is, but who. Jesus said He Himself is the manna, the bread that came down from heaven.[12] He's not only the Supplier; He is also the Supply. The best gift we could ever receive from the Father is the gift of His Son.[13] Having Him, we have everything we need.[14] Ultimately, what we need most isn't more stuff or truth or principles or resources, but more of Jesus.

God speaks a very significant truth to His people in the Old Testament through Jeremiah the prophet. He says, "My people have committed two sins: they have forsaken me, the spring of living water, and have dug their own cisterns, broken cisterns that cannot hold water" (Jeremiah 2:13). Catch this: The issue is not simply that the people turned away from the wonderful river (the bountiful supply of a relationship with God). It is that they also preferred their own cisterns (the best life they could produce apart from God) over The River, even though their cisterns were broken and could not satisfy.)

He's not only the Supplier; He is also the Supply.

"Receiving" Jesus Christ doesn't end when we accept Him

---

12. **John 6:32–35,** Jesus said to them, "I tell you the truth, it is not Moses who has given you the bread from heaven, but it is my Father who gives you the true bread from heaven. For the bread of God is he who comes down from heaven and gives life to the world." "Sir," they said, "from now on give us this bread." Then Jesus declared, "I am the bread of life. He who comes to me will never go hungry, and he who believes in me will never be thirsty."

13. **2 Corinthians 9:15,** Thanks be to God for his indescribable gift!

14. **Colossians 3:11,** But Christ is all, and is in all.

to be our Savior. That's where it starts![15] Receiving or rejecting Jesus (for all that He is and does) is one of the most important moment-by-moment choices we make each day.

(A friend of mine described all temptation as an invitation to replace Jesus with something less than He really is.) The Bread from heaven is available to meet all our real needs. (If we depend upon anything else—any relationship, objective, activity, or possession—to fill what only Jesus can fill, we won't be satisfied, and the Lord will not be honored.)

So as we use this line as a pattern for our own times of communion and communication with the Father, it leads us directly to Jesus as the only true source of all that we really need. He deeply desires that we would eat and drink of Him. He wants us to make full use of His provision.

---

15. **Colossians 2:6,** So then, just as you received Christ Jesus as Lord, continue to live in him.

Responding

1. *In what meaningful ways have you seen that Jesus is not only your Supplier, but your Supply as well? Thank Him in prayer for the many ways He supplies for you every day.*

2. *Refer back to things the daily bread can represent. Pray that He would increase one or more of these things in your life.*

3. *Pray through some of the prayers from part 3 that relate to this line (39–47).*

Chapter 9
"Forgive Us Our Debts
As We Forgive Our Debtors..."

High in the Rockies, I was with about twenty pastors from Boulder, Colorado, at a Prayer Summit. One afternoon, as we were praying the requests of the Lord's Prayer, one man said, "Lord, when You told us to pray about forgiveness here, You told us to pray in the plural—'Forgive *us* as *we* forgive.' Is there anyone we, as Your church, need to forgive? Are there people we together have offended and whose forgiveness we need to ask for?"

The answer soon came.

The same prayer resurfaced the following morning among these men, prompting a time of deep repentance. Together they recognized that they hadn't served their city; instead they'd expected the city to serve them. They'd also spoken critically against the city's leaders rather than blessing them.

They committed to go back to serve and bless.

One day a few weeks later, a group of them made appointments to talk with several key city officials. They asked a few simple questions such as, "What's your vision for our city?" and, "What are the toughest issues you face?" (This was their way of asking for prayer requests.) And this one: "How can we serve you?"

This one day opened many doors for the city's churches to enter into effective ministry opportunities through the district attorney's office, a women's shelter, the AIDS house, and several others. It also helped improve the attitude of people in the city toward the churches.

And it was all sparked by the prayer for forgiveness in the Lord's Prayer.

Our greatest need is our need to be forgiven. Jesus came to earth not simply to be our teacher, leader, example, and friend, but to be our Savior.[1] We need saving because we've all lived a life lower than God had in mind. We've all missed the target of complete selflessness. Scripture is never more true than when it states that we've all sinned and come short of God's glory (Romans 3:23).

All of us have also been sinned against. We've all been hurt by the wrong decisions and actions of others.

When we come to the topic of forgiveness, we are at the heart of the message of the Bible. Forgiveness has two aspects: receiving it and granting it. Receiving forgiveness is God's plan for how we deal with our own sin. Granting forgiveness is His plan for how we deal with those who sin against us. In our desire to pray this prayer with meaning, let's look at these two aspects of forgiveness. As we do, you'll see that the biggest and heaviest word in this line (and probably in the whole prayer) is the word *as*.

---

1. **Matthew 1:21,** "She will give birth to a son, and you are to give him the name Jesus, because he will save his people from their sins."

   Luke 10:19, "For the Son of Man came to seek and to save what was lost."

   1 Timothy 1:15, Here is a trustworthy saying that deserves full acceptance: Christ Jesus came into the world to save sinners—of whom I am the worst.

   1 John 3:8, He who does what is sinful is of the devil, because the devil has been sinning from the beginning. The reason the Son of God appeared was to destroy the devil's work.

Understanding Forgiveness

Because there's a lot of fuzziness about forgiveness, let's l at what forgiveness is *not*.

Whether we receive it or give it, forgiveness isn't a warm feeling, nor is it the absence of negative feelings. There are times when I'm forgiven and I don't feel like it, and there are times when I forgive without feeling like it.

Nor does forgiveness remove all the consequences of wrongdoing. Being forgiven doesn't mean I won't experience negative fallout from my misconduct.

Finally, forgiveness doesn't mean an escape from correction or discipline. Forgiveness deals with the past; correction and discipline deal with the future. We discipline children so that they (hopefully) won't need to receive as much forgiveness in the future as they have in the past.

So what *is* forgiveness? I would suggest that forgiveness is choosing not to retaliate. Some say, "I don't get mad; I get even," but both parts of that are flawed. As Christians, we *are* to get mad,[2] but we're not to get even. We're always to forgive. When we sin, forgiveness says God won't get even with us; when we're sinned against, forgiveness removes the reason for me to try to get even with the other person.

Forgiveness means clearing an offender's record. This is the essence of what the Father has done for us because of what Jesus did at the cross.[3]

---

2. **Ephesians 4:26,** In your anger do not sin: Do not let the sun go down while you are still angry,

3. **Colossians 2:13–14,** When you were dead in your sins and in the uncircumcision of your sinful nature, God made you alive with Christ. He forgave us all our sins, having canceled the written code, with its regulations, that was against us and that stood opposed to us; he took it away, nailing it to the cross.

It's even a willingness to bear the scars of another. The scars in the hands of the resurrected Lord[4] are an eternal reminder that forgiveness is very costly.

It's also a willingness to pay the debt of another. Many years ago, I sold Mike my electric guitar amplifier. He didn't have all the money at the time, so he was going to make monthly payments of twenty-five dollars. After he missed a couple payments, he started to avoid me. Because my relationship with Mike was more important than the money, I sought him out and forgave him the debt. Then we enjoyed a healthy relationship again.

Nearly thirty years later, he repaired my vehicle. When I offered to pay him, he said, "Don't worry about it; it's the amplifier!" I honestly didn't remember what he was talking about until he retold me the story.

> **The essence of forgiveness is releasing someone who's guilty from a real debt.**

The essence of forgiveness is releasing someone who's guilty from a real debt. That's what God has done for us and what He calls us to do for others. But there is a surprise to this releasing. When I release another person, I find that I've been released as well. My lack of forgiveness is a greater bondage to me than anything another person can put me under. An old proverb says, "If you're suffering from a bad man's injustice, forgive—lest there be two bad men."

---

4. **John 20:27,** Then He said to Thomas, "Put your finger here; see my hands. Reach out your hand and put it into my side. Stop doubting and believe."

Forgive Us Our Debts

Jesus uses the word commonly translated *debts* to describe our sin. When we sin, we become a debtor both to God and to other people.

In every situation, conversation, and decision we face, there's at least one godly way to respond. And we have everything we need to respond that way—"everything we need for life and godliness" (2 Peter 1:3). We have no valid reason to sin.

So when we fail to respond in a godly manner—and don't implement God's provision for us—we become a debtor. Our sinful actions "borrow against" the right decisions we didn't make. Therefore, we owe a debt both to God and to the others affected. When others sin against us, they owe us a debt.

How do we normally deal with these debts? We either befriend them, condemn them, or defend them.

Sometimes we treat our sin as a special friend. We adjust our schedule, priorities, finances, and lifestyle in order to make it happy.

Sometimes we go the other way and condemn it, even publicly. We beat ourselves up and we beat up anyone who "might ever think of doing such a terrible thing."

Or we may get defensive. We adopt an I'm-only-human attitude in our effort to make ourselves look and feel better.

None of these methods really deals with the issue. They don't remove our debt.

What we need is to have that debt forgiven—released. How does it happen? How does God apply to our life the answer to our greatest need?

According to the Scriptures, the Father offers us forgiveness through a combination of four conditions. Each of these conditions has the cross of Jesus Christ looming in the background because it's only through the cross that we're forgiven. Some may feel uncomfortable with the use of the word *condition* here because we know forgiveness is a free gift. But Scripture speaks of these four conditions.

The first three—confession, walking in the light, and repentance—are fairly well understood and accepted; the fourth is not.

Confession is the most familiar condition. Many Christians memorize the apostle John's words in 1 John 1:9: "If we confess our sins, He is faithful and just and will forgive us our sins and purify us from all unrighteousness." Confession of sins simply means to agree with God that what we did was sin. No excuses. No justification. Just a straightforward, "Yes, Lord, You're right. This is sin." When we confess, He cleanses. What a wonderful truth!

In fact, this is the key to beginning a relationship with the Father through Jesus Christ. It's how you come into God's family— confessing (agreeing with God) that you have a need for Him, that He has met your need in Jesus, and that you want Him to be the Boss of your life. If you've not yet made that confession, please don't wait! Please agree with God about these things right now.

Just two verses prior to this—in 1 John 1:7—John writes, "But if we *walk in the light* as He is in the light, we have fellowship with one another and the blood of Jesus, his Son, purifies us from all sin." In some ways, this is better than verse 9. That word *purifies* is in the present tense—as long as we walk in the light, the blood of Jesus *continually purifies* us from all sin. As we live in an open relationship with Jesus, even when we sin, it will be cleansed.

Jesus preached *repentance* from sin throughout His earthly ministry.[5] It's also what the disciples preached.[6] And it's the message He wants *us* to preach. The essence of repentance is turning *from* sin and *to* God. This is not at all about a "works gospel." It is simply explaining how the gospel works.

As We Forgive Our Debtors

The fourth condition for forgiveness—and the one we tend to understand the least (or ignore the most)—is a *willingness to forgive others*. We tend to water down Jesus' words about this or find some way to make them fit into our comfort zone. But He was pretty clear about this fourth condition to our forgiveness. This will be elaborated on later.

How do we actually deal with those who sin against us, those who owe us a debt? If we just don't want to forgive, what then? Or what if we're "too hurt" to forgive?

Here's where that tiny but heavy word *as* comes into play. We're called not only to receive God's forgiveness, but also to extend that same kind of forgiveness to others—to people who've actually *sinned* against us, and not just "slipped" or overlooked something.

---

5. **Matthew 4:17,** From that time on Jesus began to preach, "Repent, for the kingdom of heaven is near."

 Luke 24:47, And repentance and forgiveness of sins will be preached in his name to all nations, beginning at Jerusalem.

6. **Acts 2:38,** Peter replied, "Repent and be baptized, every one of you, in the name of Jesus Christ for the forgiveness of your sins. And you will receive the gift of the Holy Spirit."

Let me mention three big reasons why we should forgive our fellow sinners.

First, *forgiveness is a command.* Paul is pretty specific about this, and he tells us to forgive others just as we've received forgiveness.[7]

Second, *forgiveness is an invitation.* Granting forgiveness is more of a "get to" than a "have to" because it invites us into many good things.

It's also an invitation to our own relief. If we think forgiving is hard, try *not* forgiving! Carrying the burden of unforgiveness will cripple your body and cripple your soul. Bitterness is a heavier weight than any sin anyone ever committed against you. Life is way too short to carry that kind of load.

The most dramatic changes I've seen in people's lives is the transformation that comes from granting forgiveness. To go from hanging on to an offense to releasing the offense and the offender brings great freedom.

Carol was very quiet and seemed emotionally and physically fragile. She and her husband became good friends of ours and an important part of our congregation.

Then Carol came to the point of an emotional breakdown— what she calls her "emotional heart attack." This brought her to the point at times of literally needing help just to walk.

The issue was her need to forgive her father. The church provided her with an atmosphere of unconditional love. She

---

7. **Ephesians 4:32,** Be kind and compassionate to one another, forgiving each other, just as in Christ God forgave you.

   Colossians 3:13, Bear with each other and forgive whatever grievances you may have against one another. Forgive as the Lord forgave you.

received much prayer. And she began to meditate on Scripture. Over several months, she began to hear the Lord apply His Word to her specific point of need. Finally she saw that the perfect love of her perfect heavenly Father gave her strength to accept and forgive the imperfect love of her imperfect human father.

When Carol called me and told me what had happened, I immediately noticed a change in her voice. It was stronger and clearer. The change we saw in her was not only sudden and dramatic, but long-lasting. She's now serving effectively in ministry.

Granting forgiveness is an invitation to allow the Lord to deal with the person who sinned against you. When we're still judging others, it's as though God says, "If you do, I won't. But if you don't, I will. Your call." For you and me, trying to be judge of the universe is hard, especially since we're not qualified. I'm convinced that Jesus is much better at it than I am, in every way.

Finally, it's an invitation to be like Jesus. If you have made a commitment to follow Jesus, if you have responded to His call on your life, you have longed to become more and more like the Savior. We're never more like Him than when we forgive.

The third big reason for granting forgiveness is that *it's a condition to our own forgiveness,* as we've already seen. Jesus is very serious about this. He mentions it repeatedly in the Gospels. He states it simply: "Forgive, and you will be forgiven" (Luke 6:37). And again: "When you stand praying, if you hold anything against anyone, forgive him, so that your Father in heaven may forgive you your sins" (Mark 11:25).

We're never more like Him than when we forgive.

This is the one topic in the Lord's Prayer that Jesus comes back to review and reinforce (in Matthew 6:14–15) immediately after teaching the prayer. For emphasis, Jesus states it first in the positive ("For *if you forgive* men when they sin against you, *your heavenly Father will also forgive you*") and then in the negative ("But *if you do not forgive* men their sins, *your Father will not forgive your sins*").

By far the longest (and scariest) teaching Jesus shares on this is the well-known story in Matthew 18:21–35. A certain master is owed an enormously huge amount by Servant A, who pleads with him to forgive (release) his staggering debt. The master does so. Then Servant A goes to Servant B, who owes him a very small amount, and demands full repayment. Servant B also pleads for release using the same words Servant A used to his master. But Servant A refuses any mercy. Hearing of this, the master calls Servant A into his presence, "uncancels" the debt, and sends him off to be tortured in jail.

Here's the really scary part. After telling this story, Jesus says, ("This is how my heavenly Father will treat each of you unless you forgive your brother from your heart" (Matthew 18:35). What strong words! We can't read this passage attentively without catching the profound seriousness of holding others hostage in our unforgiving hands.

I confess I can't explain exactly how this fits into the true doctrine of justification by faith alone. But I do know this: Jesus is really serious about calling us to forgive others. I want to be just as serious about doing it and calling others to do it as well.

No matter how badly you've been sinned against, the best thing you can do *for your own good* is to intentionally, quickly grant full forgiveness. If there's anyone you've not forgiven "from your heart," I encourage you to deal with this now. Don't wait. Extend forgiveness to that person right away. How do you do that?

I'm glad you asked!

How Do We Forgive?

I want to give six helpful steps for knowing the joy and freedom of granting forgiveness.

Remember the offense. It's not "forgive and forget," but "remember and forgive." We don't even have the capacity to forget something at will. And if we do forget without forgiving, this only deepens both the pain and the problem. When we forgive, we'll remember the wrong that happened, but we'll also remember that we've forgiven it.

Recognize the action as sin. As a culture, we've wandered away from the word *sin*. But Jesus doesn't forgive mere mistakes or bad habits; He forgives sin. It's healthy and right to recognize what took place as a sin toward you. This shouldn't shock us—we live in a world full of sinful people (including you and me). So recognize the offense for what it is. But recognize it as a sin primarily against God, not you. When I've done this, I've found my natural response turning from anger (over my own hurt) to grief and sorrow (because of the damage to God's heart).

Remember the cross. Just as the cross is the solution for *my* sin, it's also the solution for *this* sin. Jesus left heaven and ended up on a cross because of how *I* treated Him; *I* am the "big bucks" debtor of Jesus' parable in Matthew 18. (If Jesus can forgive me of my sins, certainly I can forgive anyone for any offense against me.) The weight of my sin on the cross is heavier than the weight of any sin ever committed against me.

Release it. This is the essence of forgiveness—releasing the other person of any debt I think he owes me. Take a stamp, dip it in the blood of Jesus, and stamp the words "Paid in Full" across the old debt. This is what Jesus did for us. Also, determine not to pursue any punishment of the offender since there's no longer a debt. You've chosen to pay the debt on their behalf, just as Jesus did.

Reverse it. Jesus calls us to repay good for evil and "bless those who curse you" (Luke 6:28). Again, this is an opportunity to actually be like Jesus. Instead of focusing on the wrong action of another, focus on the privilege of becoming a little bit more like the Master. Scars can be a reminder of either the wound or the healing. Use them to remind you of the forgiveness you've granted.

Reapply it. Granting forgiveness is both an act *and* a process. Continually remind yourself that you're walking through a process. Don't expect your feelings to catch on quickly. They've been trained for quite a while to respond in a negative way when you think of this person or this action. Don't let those feelings turn you away from the real act of forgiveness. Keep reapplying it, and sooner or later your feelings will get the picture.

But what about the person who offended us who doesn't want or seek our forgiveness? How should we respond to them? Jesus says in Luke 17:3 that we're to forgive our brother "if he repents." What if he doesn't repent?

Here again, God is our model. How has He dealt with us? He has *already* done everything necessary to forgive us long before we sought it, long before we even recognized our need: "*While we were still sinners,* Christ died for us" (Romans 5:8). He has already extended forgiveness to us, though that forgiveness isn't complete until we ask for and receive it.

Both sides have a part in forgiveness: The offender asks for it, and the offended one grants it. Our part is simply to do *our* part, not theirs. If we've been sinned against, we extend forgiveness; if we're the offender, we ask for it. I can determine only my own actions and not the response of another. "If it is possible," Paul says, "as far as it depends on you, live at peace with everyone" (Romans 12:18). My freedom and peace are not determined by another person's response, but by my own action or lack of action. What wonderful news!

Let's bring this back to the Lord's Prayer. Jesus knew that one of the most powerful assets we can have as we pray is a clean heart before the Lord.[8] He wants us to enjoy the wonderful privilege of a *blameless walk*[9] as we stand before Him with *clean hands and a pure heart*.[10] He wants you to be free to approach Him in prayer without

---

8. **Psalm 66:18,** If I had cherished sin in my heart, the Lord would not have listened.

9. **Psalm 15:1–2,** LORD, who may dwell in your sanctuary? Who may live on your holy hill? He whose walk is blameless and who does what is righteous, who speaks the truth from his heart.

10. **Psalm 24:3–4,** Who may ascend the hill of the LORD? Who may stand in his holy place? He who has clean hands and a pure heart, who does not lift up his soul to an idol or swear by what is false.

the restraints of bitterness and unforgiveness shackling you. Being forgiven and extending forgiveness are essentials for this.

So I beg you to see both receiving forgiveness and granting it to others as an opportunity, not an obligation. It's a *get to* more than a *have to.*

Responding

1. As you consider the conditions of forgiveness, ask the Lord to forgive you of any and all sin.

2. Remembering the weight of the word as, *in prayer extend forgiveness to anyone who has sinned against you.*

3. Pray through some of the prayers from part 3 that relate to this line (48–50).

Chapter 10
"Lead Us Not into Temptation…"

As much as any line in this prayer, the words *lead us not into temptation* push us to understand more of what prayer actually is.

At first glance, this part of the prayer may seem to arise from fear that a dastardly God is trying to tempt us. If we'll only pray hard enough and pray "just right," He may change His mind, and we'll make it through another day of life's journey unscathed.

But prayer isn't about trying to twist God's arm to do something He really doesn't want to do. It's about aligning ourselves with the wonderful plan of a loving God to see His will accomplished here on earth through us. And God's will and desire is that we *not* be led into situations that may cause us to turn from God to lesser options. He *wants* to lead us away from temptation. So this line is not a warning; it is an invitation to agree with God's will. Then we can watch and see how He actually does lead us away from those tempting situations.

Lead Us

Though this line talks about temptation, the primary request here is that God would lead us. And God is a wonderful leader.

After He miraculously led His people out of Egypt, they sang to Him, "In Your unfailing love You will lead the people You have redeemed" (Exodus 15:13). What an encouraging truth! God doesn't stop leading us after He redeems us. In one sense, that's really when His leadership begins. And His leadership continually expresses His unfailing love for us.

This has been particularly true in my life. He has led me. When I was a high school kid interested mostly in rock and roll music and radio, He led me to a full commitment to Himself— the best thing that ever happened to me. Later He led me from a radio school to a Bible college, while I worked at a Christian radio station. From there He led me to join the staff of the little church back where I grew up. From there He led me to help establish a new congregation in the area, and He led me to pastor that congregation for more than twenty years. After all my midlife questions had come and gone, I had no ambition but to continue shepherding this flock for the rest of my life. But then, in surprising ways, over a six-week period He clearly guided me to become the director of International Renewal Ministries, a prayer ministry the Lord has used to impact people in more than forty U.S. states and thirty nations.

At each intersection in my life, God has made His clear direction known to me, sometimes even when I wasn't looking for it. He has led me not only in decisions, but also into relationships. Since the kingdom of God is a kingdom of relationships, His best leadership in my life has led me into relationships with my wonderful family and friends. He led me to my wife and to become the father to four children, then to become a father-in-law and now a grandfather as well.

Next to His loving forgiveness, His leadership in my life is the best gift I've ever received from Him. If my own plans had been fulfilled, my life would have been significantly less than it has been, and I would have missed out on so many experiences of His unfailing love.

Leading us is God's responsibility. Our responsibility is to follow that leadership. He's quite experienced and faithful in fulfilling His responsibility. He's a proven expert at it. How about us in our part? Is our "followership" as good as His leadership?

Here's another question: As we follow Him, where will we end up? When He leads us, where does He take us?

We read in Psalm 23 that He leads us "beside quiet waters" and guides us "in paths of righteousness" for the sake of His holy name. In today's too-busy world, "quiet waters" sounds like a pretty good place. The same goes for "paths of righteousness," considering the culture of selfishness all around us.

Leading us is God's responsibility. Our responsibility is to follow.

In Galatians 5, we learn that if we "keep in step with the Spirit"—follow His leadership—we end up experiencing the life of God reflected in the fruit of the Spirit (vv. 22–25). That's another good place to be. By contrast, when we follow our own leadership instead of God's Spirit, the actual result is that we "do not do what [we] want," and our lives are instead evidenced by "the acts of the sinful nature" (vv. 16–21).

Most importantly, the best place God's leadership takes us is to a closer relationship with Jesus. As the Holy Spirit makes Him known to us[1], we end up knowing the Savior better and therefore becoming more like Him.

Using this line in prayer, we can ask Him to make His leadership clear enough for us to recognize, while also thanking Him for His proven leadership in the past.

Not into Temptation

When it comes to temptation, the question is not *if* we will be tempted, but *when*. And the answer to the *when* question is "Pretty much all the time!" Temptation is a near-constant reality, and we need to know how to deal with it in our lives.

Whatever it is that's tempting us, we can rest assured that others have faced it and made it through. Temptation, as we read in 1 Corinthians 10:13, is a "common" experience—so common that even Jesus experienced it. Hebrews 4:15[2] tells us that Jesus, during His earthly trek, experienced all the real temptations we've experienced or ever will. Just as the boat that survives the storm goes through more turmoil than the one that sinks, so also Jesus experienced much more than we've ever experienced. And He made it through every one of them without sinning.

Since this is true, it's possible for us to go through our temptation as well without sinning. "God is faithful; he will not let

---

1. **John 15:26,** "When the Counselor comes, whom I will send to you from the Father, the Spirit of truth who goes out from the Father, he will testify about me."

   John 16:14, "He will bring glory to me by taking from what is mine and making it known to you."

2. **Hebrews 4:15,** For we do not have a high priest who is unable to sympathize with our weaknesses, but we have one who has been tempted in every way, just as we are—yet was without sin.

you be tempted beyond what you can bear. But when you are tempted, he will also provide a way out so that you can stand up under it" (1 Corinthians 10:13).

The origination point of temptation is never God but is always our own evil desire: "When tempted, no one should say, 'God is tempting me.' For God cannot be tempted by evil, nor does he tempt anyone; but each one is tempted when, by his own evil desire, he is dragged away and enticed" (James 1:13–14).(The evil one will use whatever he can to tempt us, but we're the ones who give him the fodder for his cannon.)

James goes on to point out a progression toward death that starts with temptation: "After desire has conceived, it gives birth to sin; and sin, when it is full-grown gives birth to death" (v. 15). Satan wants to cause death.(Satan's plan is to take what we give him of our own evil desires, then drag us (or turn us) away from our relationship with Jesus, entice us with lies, and let that desire germinate and grow.)It reproduces and "gives birth to death"—an interesting play on words. This is the same method Satan has used ever since the Garden of Eden in Genesis 3.

In contrast to this,[3] Jesus takes our desires,[4] brings us closer to Himself,[5] presents the truth to us,[6] lets that truth germinate in our lives, and then causes it to produce resurrection life in us just as it did in His life.[7]

---

3. **1 John 3:8,** The reason the Son of God appeared was to destroy the devil's work.
4. **Psalm 37:4,** Delight yourself in the LORD and he will give you the desires of your heart.
5. **James 4:8,** Come near to God and he will come near to you.
6. **John 8:31–32,** To the Jews who had believed him, Jesus said, "If you hold to my teaching, you are really my disciples. Then you will know the truth, and the truth will set you free."
7 **Romans 6:4,** We were therefore buried with him through baptism into death in order that, just as Christ was raised from the dead through the glory of the Father, we too may live a new life.

It's important that we understand here the distinction between *temptation* and *testing*. Both involve a process, but otherwise they're drastically different. *Testing* is what Abraham experienced when God asked him to sacrifice his son Isaac in Genesis 22. He passed this test—exactly as God wanted him to. Passing the test is always what He wants for us as well.

Here are some contrasts between temptation and testing:

Temptation	*Testing*
Not initiated by God	Initiated by God
Triggered by our own evil desires	Brought about by God's desire for us to grow
Purpose: to bring us down and take us away from God	Purpose: to build us up, and bring us closer to God
Based on lies (including half truths)	Based on truth
Designed to lead to death	Designed to lead to life

After James brings up the topic of temptation, he goes on to anticipate an important question: Does God actually *want* us to be exposed to temptation and to yield to it? If that's true, His goodness must surely be questioned. So James writes this:

> Don't be deceived, my dear brothers. Every good and perfect gift is from above, coming down from the Father of the heavenly lights, who does not change like shifting shadows. He chose to give us birth through the word of truth, that we might be a kind of firstfruits of all He created. (James 1:16–18)

Are you fully convinced that God is thoroug'
Sometimes we tend to think, *God is good, but...* That's why Ja...
is so emphatic on this point and addresses it in his discussion
about temptation. God *is* good. In fact, every good thing you've
ever received in your life is from a good God. He hasn't changed
and will not change. God is good. Period.

He was good in the Old Testament. David sang of His
goodness.[8] Solomon was convinced of His goodness.[9] Some
Psalms have this as their major reoccurring theme (for example
107 and 136). Jehoshaphat's singers sang about it.[10] Ezra was
convinced of it.[11] This is the message involved in bringing the
Israelites victory in battle and also bringing the presence of God
into two temples.

And He is good in the New Testament. Jesus is the Good

---

8. **1 Chronicles 16:34,** Give thanks to the LORD, for he is good; his love endures forever.

9. **2 Chronicles 5:13,** The trumpeters and singers joined in unison, as with one voice, to give praise and thanks to the LORD. Accompanied by trumpets, cymbals and other instruments, they raised their voices in praise to the LORD and sang: "He is good; his love endures forever." Then the temple of the LORD was filled with a cloud.
    2 Chronicles 7:3, 6, When all the Israelites saw the fire coming down and the glory of the LORD above the temple, they knelt on the pavement with their faces to the ground, and they worshiped and gave thanks to the LORD, saying, "He is good; his love endures forever." The priests took their positions, as did the Levites with the LORD's musical instruments, which King David had made for praising the LORD and which were used when he gave thanks, saying, "His love endures forever." Opposite the Levites, the priests blew their trumpets, and all the Israelites were standing.

10. **2 Chronicles 20:21,** After consulting the people, Jehoshaphat appointed men to sing to the Lord and to praise him for the splendor of his holiness as they went out at the head of the army, saying: "Give thanks to the LORD, for his love endures forever."

11. **Ezra 3:11,** With praise and thanksgiving they sang to the LORD: "He is good; his love to Israel endures forever." And all the people gave a great shout of praise to the LORD, because the foundation of the house of the LORD was laid.

Shepherd.[12] He is the only One who is good.[13] He calls us to do good to those who would hurt us because that is the way He is.[14] He gives good gifts.[15] He brought us "good news."

Proverbs 19:3 reflects our tendency to doubt God's goodness: "A man's own folly ruins his life, yet his heart rages against the LORD." How interesting that we're tempted to think God is somehow responsible for the things we've messed up through our own foolishness. Actually, now that I think about it, (I don't need the evil one to lead me into temptation; I can do a pretty good job of that all by myself!)

. If we're going to pray effectively and pursue a relationship with Him through prayer, we must be thoroughly convinced that God is good through and through, all the time. He doesn't have "bad days" or a dark side. He's so good that not only does He *not* tempt us, but He also makes sure we have that "way out" of temptation as mentioned in 1 Corinthians 10:13. (His desire is that we're able to "stand up" under any temptation that may come our way.) He continually goes before us, monitoring the "temptation level" around us. Whenever it gets to the "red line," (He makes sure the

12. **John 10:11,** "I am the good shepherd. The good shepherd lays down his life for the sheep."

13. **Matthew 19:17,** "Why do you ask me about what is good?" Jesus replied. "There is only One who is good. If you want to enter life, obey the commandments."

14. **Matthew 5:43–45,** "You have heard that it was said, 'Love your neighbor and hate your enemy.' But I tell you: Love your enemies and pray for those who persecute you, that you may be sons of your Father in heaven. He causes his sun to rise on the evil and the good, and sends rain on the righteous and the unrighteous."

15. **Matthew 7:11,** "If you, then, though you are evil, know how to give good gifts to your children, how much more will your Father in heaven give good gifts to those who ask him!"
James 1:17, Every good and perfect gift is from above, coming down from the Father of the heavenly lights, who does not change like shifting shadows.

LEAD US NOT INTO TEMPTATION…

exit strategy is clearly marked. Our part is to look for that way out and follow the lighted path to the exit door.

He always does His part. Will we do ours?

Temptation and Prayer

An element of our part has to do with prayer, as we learn from watching and listening to Jesus the night before He was crucified.

Just before Jesus went to Gethsemane and entered into His strongest temptation, He told His disciples they were in the enemy's crosshairs: "Satan has asked to sift you [plural] as wheat." Then He said to Simon Peter, "But *I have prayed for you,* Simon, that your faith may not fail" (Luke 22:31-32). What a gift! Likewise when *we* face temptation, we can be certain that Jesus is doing nothing less for us: He's praying for us[16]—praying that our faith will keep our eyes fixed on Him.

Soon afterward, as they came to the Garden of Gethsemane on the Mount of Olives, Jesus told His disciples, "Pray that you will not fall into temptation" (v. 40). When facing temptation, prayer is the first weapon to use, not the last. In fact, the disciples were to use this weapon so that they wouldn't fall into temptation in the first place.

Jesus then fell to His knees. Here, at His greatest hour of trial and "anguish" (v. 44), He wasn't seeking counsel or studying; He was *praying.* And His prayer brought victory—to Him and to us. Though

---

16. Please note, both the Spirit and the Son are interceding for us. **Romans 8:27,** And he who searches our hearts knows the mind of the Spirit, because the Spirit intercedes for the saints in accordance with God's will. And **Romans 8:34,** Christ Jesus…is at the right hand of God and is also interceding for us.

Calvary is where our salvation was purchased, Gethsemane is where it was decided. Jesus had entered the Garden that night "sorrowful and troubled" and "overwhelmed with sorrow to the point of death" (Matthew 26:37–38), knowing that God's will for Him included the cross and all that it represented in bearing His Father's wrath and the weight of mankind's sins. When He came out of that Garden, He had thoroughly bowed to that will and was at peace. The difference was prayer.

> Though Calvary is where our salvation was purchased, Gethsemane is where it was decided.

Embracing and applying the truths of God through prayer is our primary weapon if we're to see victory over temptation.

This Small Window

Since all temptation is an invitation to find satisfaction in something less than Jesus Christ, our part whenever we face temptation is to turn toward Jesus. He's our best help when we're tempted "because he himself suffered when he was tempted" (Hebrews 2:18). He's not only the One who *shows* us the way out of temptation—He Himself *is* the Way.[17] He's not only the Leader, but also the Destination. So when we follow Him in the midst of temptation, we end up in a closer relationship with Him.

---

17. **John 14:6,** Jesus answered, "I am the way and the truth and the life. No one comes to the Father except through me."

   1 Corinthians 10:13, No temptation has seized you except what is common to man. And God is faithful; He will not let you be tempted beyond what you can bear. But when you are tempted, He will also provide a way out so that you can stand up under it.

When He returns, we'll be *with* the Lord forever" (1 Thessalonians 4:17), and we'll also be *like* him" (1 John 3:2). These twin truths have directed my life for many years; I've sought to be with Him and to be like Him. At His return, those two desires will be perfectly accomplished in one moment. Hallelujah! I can't wait! But even now when I'm being tempted, He's the Way, the Leader, and the Destination. I don't have to wait for His return for more progress in this desire to be with and like Him. Every time I'm tempted, there's opportunity for both these things to be more fulfilled in my life.

I'm not advocating a "bring it on" attitude regarding temptation. But to the degree that we recognize temptation as an opportunity to grow in being both with Him and like Him, the evil one's goals in tempting us will be thwarted. If every time we're tempted we end up being closer to and more like Jesus, the enemy won't be as excited about putting temptation before us.

Finally, we should realize that we have only a very small window of time to exercise victory over temptation and see the evil one defeated in our lives. We had no capacity to have victory over Satan before we were followers of Christ. There'll be no need to fight temptation after we're with Jesus in heaven. It's only now, during this short slice of time, that we're able to see the enemy lose ground in our lives as we fully enter into our Lord's victory over him. Since our time is so short for seeing this happen, let's make sure we cause him as much grief as possible.

So as we take time daily to surrender to the Father's leadership in our lives, and as we remember that we are praying to a good

God, our prayers will better reflect this part of the prayer. As we ask Him to help us find the way to be closer to and more like His Son when we are tempted, we will have greater confidence that He will hear and answer these prayers. He will show us that He is the way and that we can become more like Him even when we face temptations.

—————

Responding

1. What examples from your own experience can you use to show the difference between testing and temptation? Pray prayers of thankfulness detailing some of these ways.

2. Ask the Lord to help you to find the Way (Jesus) of escape the next time you are tempted.

3. Pray through some of the prayers from part 3 that relate to this line (51–53).

Chapter 11
"But Deliver Us from the Evil One"

For many years my family has owned beach property about twenty-five miles outside Gig Harbor. It's our place of escape and relaxation. The closest thing to a house on it is a thirty-five-foot travel trailer. There's a great view of the Olympic Mountains in the distance and community waterfront.

There's also a community lagoon. The Puget Sound tide covers and uncovers this muddy area twice a day. The water's always warmest there, and it's a great place to go "mudding." Mudding is what you would do for fun in snow on flat terrain, except you do it in mud, and it's not nearly as cold. Besides playing tag-type games and playing in the ever-changing stream, one of the favorite mudding activities is standing in one spot, shifting your weight from one leg to another, to see how deep you can sink.

When our son was in late grade school, he and his two younger cousins decided to go mudding. Marilyn and I were out for a while. When we returned and drove by the lagoon, we noticed a lot of action. In the middle of it all was our son, with water up to his chest. We soon pieced together the story. They'd been mudding and his right foot was stuck—*really* stuck. He was wearing high-top tennis shoes, and the suction was stronger than he was.

And now the tide was coming in.

His cousins had summoned help from neighbors, who were

in the water with shovels and on the water in a boat. They'd tried everything with no success. I held my breath, dropped into the water, and slid my hand down to his foot, but I couldn't get it loose either.

By now we were told that rescuers from the fire department were on the way, and they knew what to do.

By the time they arrived, water was over my son's shoulders. Frankly, I was disturbed by how much time they took to get their gear ready and get their life jackets on. That was my son out there, shivering in water that was now too close to his mouth.

When the firemen were ready, they turned on a fire hose and sprayed it about two feet from his leg. It blasted the mud away, and within moments he was delivered.

He sat a while in the fire truck, wrapped in blankets. Then he sat with us in our Bronco, parked in the summer sun, with the heater on, for another forty-five minutes. Besides the hypothermia, he was fine.

We all learned three key lessons about mudding that day: (1) Always mud with a friend. (2) Never mud with high-top tennis shoes. (3) Never mud during an incoming tide.

As I've reflected on that experience, I realize I've also learned some similar key things about deliverance from the evil one: (1) Most of the time, it can be avoided. (2) The right person with the right equipment is essential for deliverance. (3) When deliverance comes, it can take place very quickly.

The Evil One

The phrase *deliver us from the evil one* is connected to the previous one *(lead us not into temptation)* by the contrast word *but*. Primarily, deliverance is what we need when we haven't followed His lead. Just like sheep, as long as we let our Shepherd lead us, we don't need Him to act as our Deliverer. But because we don't always follow as we should, we often need a Deliverer. Anticipating our proneness to wander, Jesus told us to pray to be delivered. But His hope is that we use this part of the prayer less often today than we did yesterday.

Deliverance is what we need when we haven't followed His lead.

The best way to understand this line is in reference to being delivered from "the evil one," and not just "evil." Jesus isn't talking about a concept, but about a real being. We shouldn't fool ourselves into underestimating Satan's nature. He is indeed *the* evil one. He was not created that way. He became that way because of self-centeredness. We should never underestimate its power. It wrecks everything it touches, including us.

Satan makes human terrorists seem like kindergarten bullies. He hates with pure hatred, experiencing nothing of love. He hates God and everything God loves. He hates us—primarily because he wants to damage God by hurting those God loves. He cares about no one, not even those who profess to follow him. He will murder without a second thought.

He never plays fair. There has never been a lie spoken that he didn't initiate. Lying is "his native language," and Jesus calls him a liar and "the father of lies" (John 8:44).

He's the most experienced and most practiced of all sinners. Hell was initially created to confine him. So when Jesus said "the evil one," He meant it. All evil in this world has come from the heart of Satan. Evil is present not because God wanted it, but because the evil one wanted it (He's as thoroughly evil as God is thoroughly good.)

Deliver Us

The reason Jesus includes this line in His tutorial on prayer is that whenever we need deliverance, we cannot deliver ourselves. We need the help of a real Deliverer.

Protection from the evil one is a key request Jesus prayed for His followers in His passionate prayer in John 17.[1] It's right that our prayers—both for ourselves and for others—reflect His prayer for us in this regard.

Sometimes the deliverance we need is from those who themselves are enslaved by the evil one. Paul understood this. He asked for prayer "that I may be rescued from unbelievers" (Romans 15:31) and that he and his ministry partners "may be delivered from wicked and evil men" (2 Thessalonians 3:2). And sometimes there are special situations that require specific deliverance that is more than you can receive from this chapter. If that is the case for you or a friend, please pursue special help through a trusted spiritual leader. The point of this chapter is

1. **John 17:11–12, 15,** "I will remain in the world no longer, but they are still in the world, and I am coming to you. Holy Father, protect them by the power of your name—the name you gave me—so that they may be one as we are one. While I was with them, I protected them and kept them safe by that name you gave me. None has been lost except the one doomed to destruction so that Scripture would be fulfilled…. My prayer is not that you take them out of the world but that you protect them from the evil one."

how to pray for and walk in ongoing victory in the daily struggle with Satan.

Fight or Flight

How can we be delivered from the evil one?

We first need to understand the difference between the tempter and the temptation. Although the tempter does the tempting, we're not to respond to the temptation and the tempter in the same manner. Scripture shows us a clear difference here, although we sometimes get these responses exactly backwards.

When we face temptation, we're to "flee".[2] But when we face the tempter, we're to "fight," as Jesus did when tempted by Satan in Matthew 4:1–11. Likewise, when facing sin, we're to "run," as Joseph did in Genesis 39:12[3]. But when we face Satan, we're to "resist".[4]

Our natural response, however, is just the opposite: We want to run from Satan and resist the temptation—to flee the evil one and fight the sin.

Scripture knows more about deliverance than we do. We must learn when to run and when to fight. We're to remove ourselves from the presence of temptation, but we're told to "be strong in the Lord and in his mighty power" and to "stand your ground" when encountering the evil one and his strategy "when the day of evil comes" (Ephesians 6:10–13).

---

2. **1 Timothy 6:11; 2 Timothy 2:22,** But you, man of God, flee from all this, and pursue righteousness, godliness, faith, love, endurance and gentleness.... Flee the evil desires of youth, and pursue righteousness, faith, love and peace, along with those who call on the Lord out of a pure heart.

3. **Genesis 39:12,** She caught him by his cloak and said, "Come to bed with me!" But he left his cloak in her hand and ran out of the house.

4. **James 4:7,** Submit yourselves, then, to God. Resist the devil, and he will flee from you.

Here's a summary chart of this difference:

source	our natural response	the biblical response
temptation	resist, fight	run, flee
tempter	run, flee	resist, fight

I've found that victory over both the temptation and the tempter comes more often when I see how I'm to respond to each. Then I'm able to ask the Lord to show me when I'm to stand firm and fight the evil one and when I'm to flee from temptation.

Submission and Resistance

After recognizing this difference, we can then follow the advice in James 4:7: "Submit yourselves, then, to God. Resist the devil, and he will flee from you." We're given two specific steps to take.

The first is submitting ourselves to God. Since our failure to submit to His leadership is what triggered our need for deliverance, submission to His leadership is our first active step back to safety. Submission is not a teeth-gritting experience of one whose arm is being twisted behind his back until he calls out "uncle!" It's rather a recognition of God's wisdom and love and a joyful commitment to confidently do whatever He tells us to do.

The second step is resisting the devil. Our best example of this is Jesus Himself. Jesus did serious battle with Satan in Matthew 4:1–11. The evil one wanted to thwart God's plan for humanity's redemption before it ever got started. When Jesus faced him, He faced him head-on. He heard what the tempter said, but He also controlled the conversation. He didn't respond to the devil with logic, but with the Word of God. Three times Satan came at Him, and three times Jesus answered by quoting Scripture (see Matthew 4:4, 7, 10).

God's Word is still "living and active,"[5] and it's still the best way to resist and be delivered from the evil one. I don't mean that every time you need His deliverance, you have to quote a verse of Scripture word for word or else you're stuck. But it's a good practice to fight Satan's words with God's words. You'll greatly help yourself here by memorizing and meditating on a few key passages of Scripture, becoming ready to use them with confidence.

Some of the weapons I've used against the evil one are Romans 6:11–14; 1 Corinthians 10:13; Ephesians 1:18–20; Hebrews 4:14–16; 12:4; James 1:13; 4:7; 1 Peter 4:1; 1 John 4:4. At specific points in my journey of resisting the evil one, I've memorized and meditated upon these passages, and they've served me well. As I've meditated on them, they've conformed my motives, thought life, attitudes, words, and actions more into the image of Jesus.

I encourage you to put these truths into your mind and heart and practice using them. The more we practice, the better we get.

Another aspect of being delivered is realizing that we're not only delivered *from*

> **We're not only delivered *from* something, but also delivered *to* a destination.**

---

5. **Hebrews 4:12,** For the word of God is living and active. Sharper than any double-edged sword, it penetrates even to dividing soul and spirit, joints and marrow; it judges the thoughts and attitudes of the heart.

something, but also delivered *to* a destination. When a package is being delivered, the focus is on the destination.

So as we pray from this line, we can be assured that as our Deliverer, Jesus, wants to get us where we're supposed to be. He has promised that He'll deliver us not only to heaven,[6] but He will also deliver us to a greater level of Christlikeness and maturity between here and heaven.[7] And He can get us there safely.

---

6. Jude 1:24, To Him who is able to keep you from falling and to present you before His glorious presence without fault and with great joy.

7. Romans 5:3–4, Not only so, but we also rejoice in our sufferings, because we know that suffering produces perseverance; and perseverance, character; and character, hope.

Responding

1. *Why is it significant to know that in this line Jesus is talking about the evil one rather than evil? Ask God in prayer to give you wisdom to know how to resist the evil one and run from temptation.*

2. *Pray in a manner you learned from this chapter for someone else you know who needs more freedom from the evil one.*

3. *Pray through some of the prayers from part 3 that relate to this line (54–55).*

A Final Word

In each of these last four requests—*give us, forgive us, lead us, deliver us*—the common word is *us*.

Let me remind you again of the importance of praying this "in the plural" as it is in the instruction from Jesus. I want to be very clear about this prayer's corporate application. Praying these lines not only helps us see God's heart and our own need, it also helps us see *our responsibility to one another.* When we pray, "Lord, please give *us* today what *we* need for this day," we're also taking on a responsibility and even a commitment to see the genuine needs of God's people are met. When we pray for the Lord to "forgive *us* as *we* forgive others," we're committing ourselves to live redemptively, to be peacemakers, and to help others experience the joy of being forgiven and the joy of granting forgiveness. The same is true in asking for God's leadership away from temptation and toward Him and for His delivering us from the evil one. Praying *us* rather than *me* makes me aware of my responsibility to act as *us*.

Chapter 12
Making It Yours

A re you learning to make the Lord's Prayer *your* prayer? In this final chapter, I want to summarize for you some additional approaches on how I've used this prayer as my own. I trust these further suggestions will be helpful for you and give you increased confidence.

Praying with greater confidence can also come as we pray the final line of this prayer.

Kingdom, Power, and Glory Forever

For many who've memorized the Lord's Prayer or heard it sung, those closing words are particularly majestic: "For Thine is the kingdom and the power and the glory forever." However, though this line may "sing" better than the others, the best manuscript evidence indicates that these words weren't recorded in either Matthew or Luke's account of the Lord's Prayer.

But that doesn't mean this line has no value! For one thing, the truths recorded here are clearly biblical truths. Notice for example how this line coincides in many ways with something King David prayed near the end of his life:

> Yours, O Lord, is the greatness and the power
> and the glory and the majesty and the splendor,
> for everything in heaven and earth is yours.
> Yours, O Lord, is the kingdom;

you are exalted as head over all.

Wealth and honor come from you;

you are the ruler of all things.

In your hands are strength and power

to exalt and give strength to all.

Now, our God, we give you thanks,

and praise your glorious name. (1 Chronicles 29:11–13)

When we pray, "For the kingdom and the power and the glory belong to You," we grow in godly anticipation and confidence. Since the kingdom we pray for is *His* kingdom, we can be assured there's no better place or way to live; we're praying for the best possible solutions to this world's problems. Since the power we pray for is *His* power, we can be assured that everything that needs to be done *can* and *will* be done. And since both the kingdom and the power are His, then the glory is certainly His as well. He's the One who will receive the credit and be the center of attention.

So it's very worthwhile and beneficial at the end of our times of prayer to be reminded that the One we pray to is the One who can get things done!

The charts I'll show you in the rest of this chapter outline further approaches I take to the Lord's Prayer. I'm sure there are many more than these. My encouragement is that you won't be satisfied with this small sampling but will let the Author of the prayer continue to show you even more ways to use it.

Praying God's Purposes

In the prayer's first half, the three stated phrases about God's name, kingdom, and will are like "vertical" statements of purpose—vertical in the sense that they focus our attention directly upward toward God and His desires. Meanwhile, in the second half, the four requests represent the "horizontal" dimension of requests regarding our own needs.

Please notice that these two halves are related to each other in intricate and important ways, as the following charts indicate. In fact, if I were asked to summarize the most meaningful way to pray through the Lord's Prayer, it would be the patterns indicated in the next two charts.

This first chart shows how the three "vertical" purposes are the primary reasons the Lord wants us to pray our four "horizontal" requests:

1) Give us our daily bread… 2) Forgive us as we forgive others… 3) Lead us not into temptation… 4) Deliver us from the evil one…	*so that…*	a) Your Name will be holy… b) Your kingdom will come… c) Your will is done…	*on earth as it is in heaven.*

By connecting any of the numbered "horizontal" requests with any of the lettered "vertical" purposes, we have twelve different ways to pray from this prayer. One example: "Lord, please deliver me from the evil one so that Your name would be seen as more holy." This combines (4) with (a).

Another way to approach it is seen in a second chart:

1) Let Your name be holy... 2) Let Your kingdom come... 3) Let Your will be done...	*by...*	a) giving us our daily bread... b) forgiving us as we forgive others... c) leading us not into temptation... d) delivering us from the evil one...	*on earth as it is in heaven.*

Again, the numbered phrases can be connected with the lettered phrases in any combination, giving twelve different approaches to prayer. For example, combining (1) and (a): "Lord, please demonstrate to more people on earth today that Your name is holy by providing for us just what we need for this day."

By praying in this way we focus more on God's purposes rather than on our problems.

Thanksgiving, Commitment, and Contrast

This chart suggests ways to use the prayer to help you express personal gratitude to the Lord or hear His personal commitment to us (in the middle columns), as well as seeing (in the right column) how the truths of this prayer also help us see what we really *don't* want:

The Prayer	Expressing thanks	Hearing the Lord's commitment to us	Recognizing what we don't want
Our heavenly Father...	Thank You for Your willingness and ability to be my Father.	"I am Your Father, and I'm committed to be your Father no matter what."	Lord, I'm so grateful I'm not an orphan.
Let Your name be holy...	Thank You that Your name is a name worthy to be holy.	"My name is holy, and I want you to treat it as holy."	Lord, I don't want to make *my* name holy.
Let Your kingdom come...	Thank You that You have a kingdom that has and will come.	"My kingdom *will* come."	Lord, I don't want to see *my* kingdom come.

Let Your will be done…	Thank You that You have a will for me and others that is thoroughly good.	"My will *will* be done on earth as it is in heaven."	Lord, I don't want to be seeking to do *my* will.
Give us today our daily bread…	Thank You that You're the source of everything I need.	"I am the One who'll supply your needs."	Lord, I don't want to act as though I'm my own source.
Forgive us as we forgive others…	Thank You that You forgive us and that you call us to forgive.	"I'll forgive you, and I call you to forgiveness."	Lord, I don't want to walk in my own guilt or hold on to unforgiveness.
Lead us not into temptation…	Thank You that You're such a good leader.	"I'll lead you in paths of righteousness."	Lord, I don't want to walk toward temptation.
Deliver us from the evil one.	Thank You that You're both able and willing to deliver us from the evil one.	"I'll deliver you from all that the evil one wants to give you."	Lord, I don't want to be overtaken by the evil one.

Invitation and Response

We can also use the pattern of the Lord's Prayer to help us hear the Lord's desire and His personal invitation to us (in the second column) and as a way to respond to Him in both agreement and through specific requests (the two right columns).

Another way to see this: The second column represents what we *receive* from the Lord; the third column represents how we *realign* our heart with what He says; the right column makes a *request* in response to His invitation.

The Prayer	Hearing the Lord's desire and invitation	Agreeing with Him	Making our request
Our heavenly Father...	"I want to be your Father. Let Me be."	I want You to be my heavenly Father.	I ask that You be my heavenly Father.
Let Your name be holy...	"I want to make My name holy *to* you and *through* you. Cooperate with Me."	I want Your name to be holy on earth as it is in heaven.	I ask that Your name be holy on earth as it is in heaven.
Let Your kingdom come...	"I want My kingdom to come *in* you and *through* you. Let it come.	I want Your kingdom to come on earth as it is in heaven.	I ask that Your kingdom come on earth as it is in heaven.

Let Your will be done...	"I want My will be done *by* you and *through* you. Let it be done."	I want Your will to be done on earth as it is in heaven.	I ask that Your will be done on earth as it is in heaven.
Give us today our daily bread...	"I want to supply your deepest needs. Look to Me."	I want You to give me my daily bread.	I ask that You give me my daily bread.
Forgive us as we forgive others...	"I want you to live in the freedom that forgiveness brings. Enter it."	I want You to forgive me as I forgive others.	I ask that You forgive me as I forgive others.
Lead us not into temptation...	"I want to be the One to lead you. Follow Me."	I want You to lead me away from temptation.	I ask that You lead me away from temptation.
Deliver us from the evil one.	"I want to deliver you from all that is evil. Walk in the way of escape."	I want You to deliver me from the evil one.	I ask that You deliver me from the evil one.

Martin Luther's Method

I've also found help from Martin Luther's approach to the Lord's Prayer. He would pray each line of the prayer in four different ways: instruction, thanksgiving, confession, and petition. This chart summarizes how I've applied his method:

The Prayer	As instruction	As thanks	As confession	As petition
Our heavenly Father...	Teach me more of what it means that You're my Father and I'm Your child.	Thank You for your willingness and ability to be my Father.	Too often I don't treat You like the wonderful Father You are.	Lord, be my heavenly Father.
Let Your name be holy...	Give me a deeper understanding of Your holy name.	Thank You that Your name is worthy to be holy.	Lord, there have been times when I've treated Your name as a common name.	Lord, I ask that Your name be holy on earth as it is in heaven.
Let Your kingdom come...	Teach me more of what Your kingdom looks like and how You want it to expand here on earth.	Thank You that You have a kingdom that has and will come.	I recognize that I've tried to build my kingdom rather than Yours.	Lord, let Your kingdom come on earth as it is in heaven.
Let Your will be done...	Teach me Your will, O God, and give me a heart to do it.	Thank You that you have a will for me and others that's thoroughly good.	I've tried to convince You to do what I wanted rather than to do what You desire.	Let Your will be done on earth as it is in heaven.

Give us today our daily bread...	Show me that You're the only sufficient source for all that I need.	Thank You that You're the source of all of everything I need.	Lord, there have been times when I've turned away from Your wonderful provision.	Lord, give me today what I need for this day.
Forgive us...	Teach me the severity of my sin and the glories of Your forgiveness.	Thank You that You forgive us and that You call us to forgive.	Lord, too often I've acted as though I haven't needed Your forgiveness.	Lord, forgive me today for the times when I've missed Your mark.
as we forgive others...	Teach me the need and the privilege of forgiving others.	Thank You that I get to be like You and grant others forgiveness.	Too often I've sat in judgment of others.	Let me forgive others in the same manner as You've forgiven me.
Lead us not into temptation...	Teach me to follow Your leadership away from temptation and toward Your righteousness.	Thank You that You're such a good leader.	There are times, Lord, when I take a step toward temptation rather than a step away from it.	Lord, lead me away from temptation and toward righteousness.
Deliver us from the evil one.	Teach me more of the schemes of the evil one and Your means of deliverance.	Thank You that You're both able and willing to deliver us from the evil one.	The issue, Lord, is not Your ability to deliver, but my willingness to follow You.	Deliver me from the evil one and all of his schemes.

The Role of the Trinity in the Lord's Prayer

The Father, the Son, and the Holy Spirit are all involved in our prayers. And each has a role that's reflected in this prayer. This chart reflects some understanding of each of their roles.

Though the statements here are not written in the form of prayers, you can easily turn them into prayers by expressing thanksgiving for each of these truths, or by offering specific praise to the Father, Son, and Holy Spirit for what you see here.

The Prayer	The Father...	The Son...	The Holy Spirit...
Our Father...	is the object of the prayer.	is the author of the prayer.	is the initiator and expander of the prayer.
in heaven...	reminds us of His home and our real home.	is building a home for us.	accompanies us while we're away from home.
Let Your name be holy...	tells us the value of His name.	shows us the value of His name.	leads us to value His name.
Let Your kingdom come...	"births" us into His kingdom.	is the King of the kingdom.	guides us as we live in the kingdom.
Let Your will be done...	communicates His will to us.	accomplishes and demonstrates the Father's will for us.	leads us into the Father's will and enables us to do it.

Give us today our daily bread...	is our Provider (providing all that we really need).	is our Provision (our Daily Bread).	points us to the Provider and the Provision.
Forgive us...	grants us forgiveness.	provides the basis of forgiveness.	convicts us of our need for forgiveness.
as we forgive others...	commands us to forgive.	demonstrates how to forgive.	convicts us of our need to forgive.
Lead us not into temptation...	provides a "way of escape" from temptation.	is the "way of escape" (our example) during temptation.	leads us to and through the "way of escape" during temptation.
Deliver us from the evil one.	promises deliverance.	has ultimately defeated the evil one; He's our deliverer.	shows us the evil one and guides us away from him.

Responding

1. *After going through this book, what most convinces you of the worth and value of intentionally praying the Lord's Prayer?*

2. *What actions or changes in your life are you committed to as a result of going through this book?*

PART THREE

Prayers from the Lord's Prayer

This part of the book contains prayers based on my understanding of the Lord's Prayer. I offer them as a way of helping you implant these truths into your own prayer practice. In one sense, this is the real heart of this book; I so desire that this way of praying will become as meaningful to you as it has been to me.

In one sense, this is the real heart of this book.

I hope these prayers serve two purposes for you. First, that they'll be very meaningful to you as you pray them. Second, and more importantly, that they'll help you catch the way the Spirit of God wants to make the Lord's Prayer alive in you.

You can think of these as training-wheel prayers, assisting you until you can "ride" on your own. Or think of them as being like the free food samples offered in the supermarket. These prayers are offered in the hope that you'll go on to buy the real thing—your own immersion in the Lord's Prayer as your personal guide for a lifelong prayer journey.

1. As an Expression of Thanks
Father, I join with the psalmist and say, "It is good to give thanks to the Lord." What a privilege to come to You and express my thanks! Thank You, Father, for all You have done to let me call You my Father. Thank You for Your willingness to let me address You in such a relational manner. Thank You for Your name and

Your nature, which it expresses. Thank You that Your name is the only name that is worthy to be called holy. It is the only name given that can bring us salvation. It is the only name all people will one day recognize as the Name above all other names. Thank You that as the King, You have a kingdom that has come, is coming, and will come. Thank You that You have a will for me and others that is knowable and is thoroughly good. Thank You that You are the source of everything I have needed and ever will need. Father, Thank You that You forgive us. Thank You Jesus, for Your willingness to go to and through the cross so that I could be in Your family. And thank You, Holy Spirit, for not giving up on me when I resisted You. Thank You for Your wonderful conviction and the gift of repentance. And thank You for Your present staying power in my life. Thank You for calling me to forgive others just as You have forgiven me. Thank You that You are such a good leader. Thank You for the invitation to follow You. Your path is far better than my path! And thank You that You are both able and willing to deliver us from the evil one. Yes, it is good to give thanks to You!

2. As Our Heavenly Father, You…
As our Heavenly Father…

You have shared Your name with us by allowing us to call You "our Father." You willingly allow us and invite us to be identified with You!

You have told us about Your kingdom. You demonstrated it to us through the life of Jesus and invited us into it.

You have given us clear instructions about what Your will is and how we can see it take place. You have promised us Your provision and fulfilled Your promises.

You have offered us complete forgiveness and called us to forgive as You do.

You have shined Your light on our paths and have provided all we need to walk in it.

And You have delivered us from our own path and from the path of the evil one.

Yes, we are so thankful that You are our heavenly Father!

3. As the Lord's Will for Us

Father, I hear You say to me that...

You want to be my Father and You want me as Your child.

You want Your name to be holy to me and through me.

You have a kingdom that You want to grow in me and through me.

You want Your will to be accomplished by me and through me.

You are the trustworthy supplier of all my needs.

You have graciously released me from all my debt to You, and You want me to extend that release to others.

You want me to follow You as You lead me away from harmful decisions.

You are even willing to deliver me when I don't follow You as I should.

4. As Your Son (or Daughter)

Today, Lord I want to be a good son to You. I so rejoice that You are my heavenly Father! Please give me Your grace to live completely for You today. As I move through this day, I want to live in such a way that Your name is as revered in my home as it is at Your home. Give me Your grace to see and take every opportunity today to reflect Your holiness. I want to see more of Your kingdom established here. I look forward to the way Your grace will point out kingdom activity around me and help me fan it. And I want more of Your will accomplished here on this earth. Give me grace to be part of the accomplishment of Your plans today. My desire today is to be dependent on Your good provision. Help me to see Your means of provision and receive them. Also, Lord, I want to be as forgiving of others as You have been toward me. Give me grace to forgive fully and quickly. And I want to follow You. I look forward to walking in paths of righteousness because I have sensed and followed Your leadership. I ask for your grace to be attentive and responsive. I also know that there will be times when I will need You to deliver me from the evil one. Thanks that You have completely defeated him. I want him to have no hold on me today. Let me see his schemes, and give me grace to cooperate with You in his defeat.

5. Because You Are Our Heavenly Father, We...

Because You are our heavenly Father, we are very blessed. We get to come to a God whose name is holy, here in the midst of a world where there is so much unholiness. We rest in the reality that no matter what the circumstances may look like, Your kingdom is coming. We rejoice that in the midst of all that is not Your will, Your will is being and will be done. We receive the loving provision from Your hands and heart. We receive Your gracious forgiveness and therefore joyfully release all those we think may owe us a debt. We accept Your leadership over us and in all the situations we may face today. And we look for the ways You have brought us and will bring us Your deliverance.

6. It Is Good…

You are good, and everything You do is good. Lord, it is good to come to You and address You as "Our Father." It is good that You are my "heavenly" Father, not just a very good earthly one. It is good that Your name is holy and that You are being known more and more as holy here on earth today. Your kingdom is good, and it is good that it is coming to earth today. Your will is good, and it is good that it is being done here today. Your daily bread is good. It smells good, tastes good, and is good for us. Your forgiveness is also so good. Yes, it is so good to know that You are not counting my sins against me! And it is good that You call us to forgive others. You are such a good leader. Both the process and the destination of Your leadership are good. It is also good that You provide a way of escape when we don't follow You. So the way You deliver us from the evil one is also very good.

7. Lord Let Me…

Our—Lord, let me be more aware of the corporate nature of my walk with You today.

Father—Lord, let me be a good son to You. Lord, let me be responsive to and respectful of what You say.

In Heaven—Lord, let me be more aware of Your character and my destination. Lord, let every decision I make today reflect both of them.

Let Your name—Lord, let me be more concerned about Your name, character, and reputation today than mine.

Be holy—Lord, let me reflect Your holiness in all my motives, attitudes, thoughts, words, and actions.

Let Your kingdom come—Lord, let me cooperate with You to see as much as possible of Your kingdom be established and strengthened.

Let Your will be done—Lord, let me fulfill Your highest will by loving You and others fully today.

On earth as it is in heaven—Lord, let me be a conduit so that more of heaven is on earth today because I have lived as Your child.

Give us this day—Lord, let me receive all that You want to give me today, and make it available to those You put in my path.

Our daily bread—Lord, let me especially receive more of the "Bread that comes down from heaven."

Forgive us our debts—Lord, let me be quick to acknowledge my sins so I can receive Your forgiveness.

As we forgive our debtors—Lord, let me also be quick to fully forgive anyone who sins against me.

Lead us not into temptation—Lord, let me be a good follower of You today so that I can always see Your way of escape.

But deliver us from the evil one—Lord, let me be so close to You today that Your enemy and his schemes have no influence on me whatsoever.

8. *You...*

I am grateful, Lord, that You have invited us to come and pray to You, not someone lesser, but directly to *You*. I don't need to come to a god who doesn't care or to a god who may care but can't see or act. I get to come to *You*! I get to come to the One True God, who is both able and willing to hear and answer my prayers.

You are my heavenly Father. *You* have a name that is holy. *You* have a name that deserves to be seen as holy here in our world. *You* have a kingdom. *You* are causing that kingdom to come and grow here on earth. *You* have desires You want to see accomplished here in my home and my hometown, and *You* are active in accomplishing those desires today.

You are the One who regularly supplies all I need. *You* offer us forgiveness in Jesus Christ. *You* call us to forgive, just as *You* do. *You* are the Leader leading us away from temptation and leading us toward Yourself. *You* show us where it is safe to step. And *You* are the Deliverer. When we wander into trouble, *You* are the one who finds us, fixes us, and frees us.

The following prayers are taken from the entire prayer applied to various specific settings.

9. A Business Owner's Version

Heavenly Father, today as I represent You through the business You have given me, help me find that balance between relating to You as a wonderful Father and standing in awe of You as the One in heaven. Help me use the avenue of this business as a means to let others know that there is none like You, that You alone are holy. Let me see and take opportunities to build Your kingdom, not simply my business. Let me know that it is not simply about how I direct the lives of others, but about how You are seeking to direct my life. Let me demonstrate to my employees and my customers what it means to do Your will here on earth.

I look to You as my supplier. I recognize that all I have has come from You. You have given me everything I need for life and godliness. You have given me everything I need to honor You in the market You have provided. Help me to apply what You have given me to the situations I face today. Let healthy relationships grow in this place. Let forgiveness flow whenever and wherever needed, beginning with me. Keep me from being tempted to think that it is more about money than about influencing others for You. And in the midst of all the decisions I make and interactions I have today, keep me protected from the evil one and all his desires and schemes.

10. A Congregational Version

Heavenly Father, today I pray for the saints in our congregation. I join with Your desire that we see You as a loving Father and ourselves as children of light. You have invested so much to bring us into Your family. Please let us give You a good return on Your investment. Let us be holy as You are holy. Let Your name be holy to each person in our congregation today. Let them reflect that holiness to others so that You are more respected in our world. And let Your saints be more aware of and receptive to Your kingdom ways. Give them hearts to seek Your kingdom, eyes to see it and hands to serve it. Let them accomplish Your will in whatever situation they're in today. Let them love well in old ways and also new ways.

Please provide for them all they need. Give them what they need in the physical realm, the financial realm, the emotional and relational realms, and especially the spiritual realm. But especially, give them more of Yourself today. Give them a sensitivity toward sin so that they acknowledge it and turn from it quickly. Forgive them and help them forgive others who sin against them. Then lead them as the True Shepherd leads His sheep. Take them away from things that would harm both You and them, and take them toward You. And when they follow a path that would damage them and You, deliver them. Bring them back safely, and let them learn because of the experience.

11. A Parent's Version
Father, as I come to You today, I am so grateful that You are the best Father ever! You, more than anyone else, know how to parent a child. Thanks for Your example. Now I need Your help. Help me demonstrate Your holy name to my child(ren) today. Help me, by my decisions and behavior, to instill in them a sense

that You are not like anyone or anything else. Allow me to be kingdom-minded today. Help me to bring righteousness, peace, and Holy Spirit joy to their lives and this house because I am walking in these things. Let them see me loving You and them in ways that will lure them to do Your will as well.

You have been such a good provider for this family! You have provided all that we need and many things we don't need. Let the abundance of Your provision produce gratitude in my child(ren) rather than more expectations. We also acknowledge that we need Your forgiveness. Help me to grant forgiveness to others in my family as well as to ask forgiveness from them. Let Your forgiveness be applied to each of our lives as often as needed, but let it be needed less today than yesterday. Please lead us into more and more of Your life for us. Lead us away from temptation and toward Your Son. And finally, keep us from the evil one, and when we don't follow Your path, please be especially gracious to us and intervene in his schemes against us.

12. A Christmas Version

We recognize, Father, that the event we celebrate this morning is the event that made You *the* Father so that You could be *our* Father. Today we embrace You more fully as our heavenly Father. The name You chose for Your Son was a fairly common name, but He was anything but common! He was the first and only One who was able to completely demonstrate that You are the One Who Saves. Today and this year, please let us demonstrate the holiness—the uniqueness—of the name "Jesus." On this day we also ask again that just as Jesus (the King of the Jews) came, may He and His kingdom come more and more into our world every day and into our everyday world. Just as Jesus left heaven to come to our world to do the will of the Father, may we also live our lives fully willing and committed to do the same.

The fact that You gave us (this day) the Bread that comes down from heaven gives us deep assurance that You will continue to give us all the other "bread" we need. This morning, we are reminded that He came from heaven to earth not only to teach us, heal us, and inspire us, but also to forgive us. Forgive us of our sins. And let us forgive others as fully as we ourselves have been forgiven. Lead us today, not only in the little steps, but lead us in the big picture of our life as You see it. Let us willingly follow the same pattern as His life. Let us be willing to leave our "perfect place" in order to do Your will in the place of Your choosing, even when we may be rejected and even when it may cause us great pain. And since You came to deliver us from and to destroy the works of the evil one, let us see and join You in this fight, so Your kingdom, power, and glory may become far more evident in our world than they are this Christmas morning.

13. A New Year's Day Version
Father, as I look back, it is very clear to me that this past year You have again been a wonderful Father to me. Now, this year let me be a better son to You. Let me live my life this year in such a manner that Your name is seen as holy to more people in my world. Let more people know how sacred You really are. This

year, please let more of Your kingdom come to my family and to all those I have contact with. Let there be more righteousness, peace, and joy in this world because of the way I walk with You. And let Your will be more accomplished this year than last year. Let me love You and others more this year than last year. Let Your love be more evident to me and through me.

Continue to provide for me this year. May I be more aware that all I have really does come from Your good hand of provision. Give me grace to forgive others more fully and quickly. And give me grace so my need for forgiveness from You is less this year than last year. I look forward to Your leadership of my life again this year. Increase my capacity to know and follow Your leadership. And You are such a good deliverer. Keep me protected from the evil one and all of his schemes by keeping me in the tower of the strong name of Jesus.

14. A Good Friday Version

As we come to You on this day, Father, we are aware of only a small part of the pain Your heart experienced because of the suffering of Your Son. Jesus, the extent You were willing to go to demonstrate the holiness of Your Father's name is just amazing! I cannot grasp Your willingness to surrender and suffer in order to bring His kingdom. The pain that Your commitment to His will brought You causes me to stand in awe!

Oh, Lord Jesus, this wonderful act of love brought the greatest provision to the greatest need! Your death is what allowed the Father to say and what motivates me to say to others, "You are forgiven!" It more than anything else makes me flee any and all temptation. And it is the ultimate statement of Your defeat of and my deliverance from the evil one! Thank You so much for Your love displayed by the cross. I receive it!

15. An Easter Version

This day we enter into Your joy, Father, at the resurrection of Your Son! We rejoice that because He is alive, He has demonstrated the holiness of Your name, established Your kingdom, and accomplished Your will! Assist us, the body of Your Son, to complete what He has begun. Please help us to respond to Your Spirit so that we would do what Jesus did and keep doing what Jesus is now doing in answer to these requests.

Because of His resurrection, we have received all we need. Let us use the provision, the forgiveness, the leadership, and the deliverance we have received from You to cooperate with You in seeing the complete fulfillment of Your plans, which You began to unfold at the empty tomb and are still affecting us today!

16. An Ascension Day Version

Today, heavenly Father, we enter into Your joy and the joy of Your Son as we consider this day when Jesus, after His birth, life, death, and resurrection, ascended to You in great triumph! This day, as You made His enemies a footstool for His feet, You proved again that You alone are the One worthy to be called holy. It proved that Your kingdom had been established and would be brought to fulfillment. It proved that Jesus had done Your will by completing His earthly work.

Now, as He intercedes for His church, we join Him and say, "Yes, give them today what they need today and each day." And let them apply the blood that has been applied to Your altar to all the areas of their life so they may receive Your forgiveness. As they rejoice at how You have forgiven them, let them follow You by forgiving others. Lead them in paths of righteousness so they may be so delighted in Your exaltation that they have no time, need, or desire to turn away from You toward temptation. And as we celebrate Your complete victory over the evil one, remind us that even though the outcome of the battle is determined, it is not over yet, and we still need Your deliverance and protection.

The following prayers are taken from a word or a phrase of the prayer.

17. Our

Heavenly Father, I recognize that the first thing Jesus taught us about prayer is the value of praying in the plural. And He reinforced it through the use of the word *us* in the second half of this prayer. Help me to grasp this.

Thank You that prayer is not simply an individual sport. I get to come to You as one member of Your body, of my family, of my congregation, of the church of my city, of my company, of my community, etc. I am grateful that You have told me I cannot say to the other members of Your body, "I don't need you," nor can I say, "You don't need me." Continue to show me how valuable the body is to me and how valuable I am to the rest of the body.

Help me see Your bride only as You see her. Show me and others around me how valuable our unity is to You, to us, and to the world around us. And show us how dangerous it is to the kingdom of darkness. Then please help me to be a catalyst always for unity in the body of Christ and never for division.

Also, Lord, give me opportunities to pray this prayer with others. Increase my desire, capacity, and opportunity for meaningful and effective times of corporate prayer.

18. Our (2)

As I come to You this morning, Father, I again recognize that You are not simply my Father, but *our* Father. I acknowledge that You delight in the relationship You have with so many others. So today, even though I so cherish Your relationship with me, please make me more and more aware of the ways You cherish Your relationship with so many of the others in the *our* part of this prayer.

Allow me to enter into the same kind of care for others as You have. Increase my awareness of Your great, unsurpassing love and care for all of Your family. Open my eyes today to see how much You care for others in Your family. Show me some of the specific ways You want to care for them. Then open my eyes to see how I can be part of Your care for them. Let me be a good assistant for You today. I want to sign up as a distributor of Your love. Help me be a good bucket, carrying Your love and care to those You care deeply about. Help me to be an envelope carrying a letter of Your love delivered to the correct address at the correct time.

19. Father

Father, there are so many titles and names by which You could and should be addressed. You are the Creator. You are the Most Holy One. You are the Lord of lords. You are the King of kings.

You are the Captain of the heavenly armies. You are the Infinite One. You are the Ruler of heaven and earth. You are the One who lives in unapproachable light.

Every time we come to You in prayer, it is appropriate for You to ask us to address You by one of these titles. It would be right if You required us to address You as "The Most Holy One," "Master," or "The Almighty One." But when Jesus taught us to approach You, He told us to call You our Father. What a wonderful invitation! To be able to address the God of the universe in one of the most relational terms in our language makes coming to You even more of a delight. You are all those things listed above, but above all of them, You are my "Papa," my "Daddy." Just like the child whose father owns the company, You may have many titles, but Your best name to us is Daddy! Thank You that You always welcome us and never turn us aside because You are too busy with other, "more important" things.

I am so thankful I can look to You and call You my Father!

20. *Our* Heavenly *Father*

Oh, Father, how good it is to approach You knowing that You are not simply a good earthly father, but You are our *heavenly* Father. Some of us had fathers who did a pretty good job in reflecting Your character and Your ways to us. But others of us had fathers who simply did not reflect a very accurate picture of You at all. Either way, there is more of You to know than what any earthly father could show us.

But whether our dads did a good job or not, You delight not

only in repairing us, but also in reparenting us. As I look to You, please fill out or fill in the places in my heart where I need a better picture of who You actually are.

Come, Lord Jesus, and show us more of the Father. Show us more of His ways, His heart, His hurts, His plans, and His desires. Help us to know Him more so we can trust Him better. As our heavenly Father, lift up our eyes so we look at and think about the things that matter most to You. Help us to contemplate our heavenly Father more so that we can be better earthly children.

21. Son (or Daughter)

Thank You again, Father, that I get to be Your son today. As Your son I want to live up to the family name. You have said that "a good name is more desirable than great riches." And Your name deserves the best reputation ever! Don't let me do anything today that will damage Your reputation. I know that it is not simply what I say but primarily what I do that will affect how people view Your name today. So let my actions reflect Your actions. It is Your will that I imitate You as I interact with people today. You want me to handle conversations and situations just as You would. Help me to imitate You well. I want to watch You; I want to keep an eye on how You do things so I can do them just as You do. Help me to be a good son today by representing You and Your family well.

22. Privileges of Being Your Son (or Daughter)

Father, how you have lavished Your love on me! You allow me to be known as Your son, because that is what I really am! This morning, I want to tell You again that this makes all the difference in the world to me. I receive Your love for me today. Please help me recognize it and receive it in whatever form You choose to give it to me today. Whether it is in a very familiar manner or in a manner I would never expect, let me see it and respond well to it. I also thank You that because I am Your child, You have sent the Spirit of Your Son into my heart, and I get to call you "Papa." I no longer need to act like a slave; I get to act like a real son. I also have a newfound freedom! Thank You that You have liberated me from bondage and I get to live apart from fear. Also, I am so grateful that even though I don't understand all of what it means, I get to be Your heir. I get to receive the hope of eternal life because I am Your son. Thank You so much, Lord, for the privileges I have because You have made me Your son. I receive them and rejoice in them.

23. Responsibilities of Being Your Son (or Daughter)

Father, today, I reaffirm that with the privileges of being Your son also come significant responsibilities. Even though these are beyond my human, fleshly ability to fulfill, I know I am responsible to allow Your Spirit to direct and empower me doing so. Please help me today to reflect Your character, not simply when it is easy or it makes sense, but in those times when it seems impossible or it doesn't make any sense. Give me grace to respond in the opposite spirit to those who would be my enemy or would persecute me or would speak against me. Help me to love them like You do—because You do.

Today You have called me to be holy just like You are. I accept that responsibility. Let every aspect of my life be different because You have made me different. Remind me of my new life in You, and allow me to follow You today. Make me more sensitive to the promptings of Your Spirit so I will know how and where He is leading me. Let me see the good deeds He is preparing for me to walk in, and then let me keep in step with Him.

Give me that childlike excitement that says, "When I grow up, I want to be just like Daddy!" Help me be as excited about the responsibilities of being Your child as I am about the privileges of being Your child.

24. Your

Father, I am so grateful that You address my deep addiction in this prayer. It seems I am hopelessly and helplessly addicted to myself. Clearly, the default setting of my life is my name, my rule, my will, my sufficiency, my forgiveness, my leadership, and my deliverance. Even when I pray, I find my prayers are way too filled with both subtle and serious statements of selfishness. Please forgive me. After years of intentionally walking with You, it seems it shouldn't be this way! I have consciously embraced my dependence on You, but I still say with Paul, "Oh, wretched man that I am! Who shall deliver me?" God, I am so thankful that in this prayer You drag me from self-centered praying and living to God-centered and other-centered praying and living. Thank You for not only showing us the priority of Your name, Your kingdom, and Your will, but for also forcing us to deal with these truths regularly. I so need this intentional, regular readjustment of my thinking, decision-making, motivation, and living. Continually starve this addiction as I again, this morning, declare that today is all about Your name, Your kingdom, Your will, Your supply, Your forgiveness, Your leadership, and Your deliverance.

25. Let Your Name Be Holy

Father, as I come to You this morning, I am so grateful that You have revealed Yourself in Your holy name. I agree with You that Your name is and should be seen as holy in and through my life today. Let me live in such a way that my life causes me and others to treat Your name in a more holy manner. Both Your character and Your reputation are reflected in Your name. Let me live consistently with Your character. As I move through the events and contacts of this day, let me know more of Your character and also demonstrate it in the midst of those events and contacts. Your reputation is the only one that really matters. As I understand more of You today, let me know more of the value of Your reputation, and also let me treat it with the utmost respect. Show me the contrast between the value of my reputation and the value of Yours. I look forward to how You can and will use this day as another day of training me to treat Your name as the one that really is the Name above all names.

26. Let Your Name Be Holy (2)

This morning, Father, I recognize that You are so very holy. But I also recognize that You did not become holy because You were good, but You are good because You are holy. I recognize that the essence of holiness is that You are different from everyone and everything else. There is no one like You! And just as You did not become better and better and then at some point become holy because You were so good, so also I recognize that my part in reflecting Your holiness is not a matter of getting better and better. I receive the reality that my holiness is not based on my capacity to become better and better, but rather on Your decision to set me apart for Yourself and Your service. So as I seek to see Your name as holy, help me today to simply live as though I am really different from what I used to be. Help me see that You have imparted something to me that is far more than putting a new coat of paint on a rusty old car. You have actually made me a brand-new model! Today I receive Your work of holiness in me. I receive the newness of life You have given me. Now, because I am a "new creation," please let me live this day consistently with that newness of life. Don't let me live like I am *not* different, but let me live like I really *am* different.

27. Yahweh *Is Holy*

Father, I praise You that You have revealed Yourself to us! Specifically, I praise You because You have revealed Yourself to us through the name of Yahweh. Your Word tells us that You want to be known through Your name and that You are jealous to protect Your name. Today I want those things as well. I want to know You more as the great "I AM." And through all that I do today, I want to represent Your name well.

I know some of what Your name means, but I want to have a greater awareness that *You are* with me throughout this day. Help me have a better grasp that *You are* not only all I need, but that *You are* everywhere I am. There is no one else I can say that about. *You are* the only one who is all I need and always available. The truth is, "There is none like You!" Help me act like that today. Help me live as though *You are* there, with me in every situation and conversation. Let everything about me—my motives, my attitudes, my thoughts, my actions, and my words—communicate to other people that *You are* truly in the midst of us.

Lord, it is an awesome thing to be trusted to represent Your name. I so often have misrepresented You! I don't want to misrepresent You today! Today, as I rely on You, let me live what the psalmist expressed when he said "Whom have I in heaven but You? And earth has nothing I desire besides You."

28. Jesus *Is Holy*

Father, I praise You for the name of Your Son, Jesus! Even though it was a very common name, He is anything but common! Today, let me treat the name of Jesus differently from the way I treat all other names.

I praise You that through this name You have shown Yourself to be a God who cares! Gabriel told Joseph, "You are to give Him the name Jesus because He will save His people from their sins." His name shouts "Savior" at us! Today, I want Jesus to be my savior, not only from the penalty of sin, but also from its power! Help me rely on His strong name, His strong character, and His strong promises, and let Him be my Savior in very practical ways. Let everything about me reflect the fact that I am looking to Jesus to be my Savior. Let my decisions, interactions, conversations, words, thoughts, and everything else about me demonstrate that I am relying on Jesus to show that He cares for me more than anyone else does or can care for me.

As Hebrews 2:11 says, "Both the one who makes men holy and those who are made holy are of the same family. So Jesus is not ashamed to call them brothers." So let me live in such a way that Jesus would not be ashamed of anything I do because the One who is holy is making me more holy.

29. Receiving the Kingdom

Father, this morning, with a heart of anticipation, I pray that Your kingdom would come in greater measure here on earth just as it has come in heaven. Specifically, I ask that Your kingdom would increase in my life today. I again set my heart on the priority of seeking Your kingdom before I seek other matters. I welcome the coming of Your kingdom in me and through me. Let me see that Your kingdom is more valuable than all my other possessions. Remind me, throughout today, that it is worth selling everything to possess.

Lord, since Your kingdom comes to those who are poor in spirit, let me be deeply aware today that I have nothing I can use to buy it from You. Since it sometimes comes through hardships and persecutions, I ask that today, You would allow me to see that hardships may be what You use to answer this prayer. Since You have said that repentance is necessary to enter into Your kingdom, give me a heart that is ready to turn toward it every time I see it. But whatever ways You present Your kingdom to me today, let me recognize it and let me receive it!

Yes, Lord, let Your kingdom come in me. And let me be a carrier of Your kingdom. I ask that it would increase in me and also that it would flow through me to others. In a world where it seems like Jesus is not really ruling, let me be evidence that He is ruling in my life and through my life to others.

30. His Kingdom Is Righteousness, Peace, and Joy

Lord, You have said much about Your kingdom. Again, today, I want more of Your kingdom to come in me and through me. Since Your kingdom consists of righteousness, peace, and Holy Spirit joy, I open my life and ask for more of these kingdom traits.

God, please increase the level of Your righteousness in me and through me. Convince me that I really do stand before You in the righteousness of Jesus Christ and that therefore I don't have to try to justify myself! Then allow me to do my part in having right relationships with all those I will come in contact with today—those I know well and those I have not yet met.

Grant me more of Your gift of *shalom*. Let me take full advantage of the peace Jesus fought to establish between us at the cross. Let me come to it, and let it come to me. Let it rule my heart and my mind. Increase peace in me by increasing my love for Your law. Today, let me grow as both a man of peace and a peacemaker.

Finally, let me walk in that righteousness and peace in the joy of Your Holy Spirit. Let Your joy be my strength today. Increase my awareness and confidence that my joy does not rest in what happens to me or around me but rather in Your loving sovereignty. Let me fully embrace Your known and as yet unknown plans for my life this day with the anticipation of a young child on Christmas and watch You work out the details.

31. The Kingdom Parables

Jesus, You seemed to always be looking for ways to describe Your kingdom to Your disciples. Many times You took a kingdom truth and connected it to something Your disciples were very familiar with. Help me to have eyes for Your kingdom as You did.

I want to learn the kingdom lessons You taught Your disciples. Since Your kingdom comes through words, let me have ears to hear what Your Spirit is saying to me, even though it may come through a source I am not familiar with or a source I don't even like! Since the soil determines how the seed grows, make my heart good soil. Please remove any rocks and pull up any thorns so that nothing hinders the long-term growth of Your Word in me. Give me a clear understanding that You have an enemy who will be trying to undo what You do in me. Protect me from him and his bad seed. Then let the size of Your kingdom, no matter how big it is in me at this point, grow and become larger and larger. I want the inherent growth capacity of the kingdom to have its way in me. And let Your kingdom not stop growing in me until it permeates every aspect of my life. Let it affect everything about my family, my work life, my hobbies, and all my relationships. Show me how valuable Your kingdom is to me and also how valuable I am to it. Finally, please show me that it is not up to me to judge or determine who is or is not in Your kingdom. You are the One who can do that best.

32. The Kingdom from Mark 4:26–29

Father, again I ask that Your kingdom would come in me and through me to a world that needs Your kingly rule. As much as I can, I want to cooperate with You in this process. But I also recognize that it is not simply about what I do. You have told us a very interesting story about how Your kingdom grows. I want to respond well to these truths as well.

Let Your kingdom come in me during the day, when I am active, and also during the night, when I am asleep. Let it sprout and grow whether I get up or sleep. Even when I don't know how it is growing, please let it grow "all by itself." And let it grow in Your divine order, "line on line," so that the end result is Your result, not mine. Then also, Lord, in Your timing, put Your sickle into my field and let the harvest of my life produce a crop that will nourish others and glorify You.

33. The Kingdom from Colossians 1:12–13

Heavenly Father, I am so grateful that You have qualified us to share in the inheritance of the saints in the kingdom of light! Thank You that we did not qualify ourselves but that You qualified us. And thanks that part of our inheritance is that we get to live right now in the kingdom of light. You rescued us from the domain of darkness, and You brought us into the kingdom of Your beloved Son! What a change You have made in us. What a privilege to live in a whole new realm.

Since You have done this on our behalf, would You now allow me, my family, my congregation, and all of Your body to live as though that were really true! Help us to no longer grope along as though we were still in the darkness. Help us to no longer bow to what we used to bow to. Help us to live lives of transparency before You and others.

Help us to live as though we really are in the kingdom of Your beloved Son. Increase our passion to know the King, be with the King, obey the King, and love the King! Even though we may never forget the former king and kingdom, let the reality of the new King and the new kingdom dominate our thinking and therefore our lifestyle so much that the former becomes simply a distant shadow compared to the new brilliant light.

34. The Kingdom from Revelation 11:15 and 22:17, 20
Father in heaven, I really am delighted to know that Your kingdom is both "here and now" as well as "there and then." I so rejoice that I no longer have to live in the domain of darkness, but I get to have Your kingdom come and grow in me and make me more like the Savior.

But I also recognize that the best we experience of the present kingdom is only a partial expression of the full coming kingdom. And the kingdom will not fully come until the King comes again.

Therefore, I join with saints throughout the world and throughout the ages and pray, *Lord, let Your ultimate kingdom come to this world.* We long for the time when "the kingdom of this world has become the kingdom of our Lord and of His Christ, and He will reign for ever and ever!" We join our voice with the Spirit and the rest of the bride and say, "Come." We join with John as he considered the hell-on-earth he anticipated before he would see You again and, determining it was worth any amount of suffering he would go through, cried out, "Even so, come, Lord Jesus!"

Since we will never experience ultimate righteousness on this earth without the King of righteousness, since we will never have full peace without the Prince of Peace, since we will never know complete joy without the Source of Joy, and since we will never experience the full kingdom without the presence of the King, we call out to You and say, "Yes, Lord, please come quickly. Let the bride make herself completely ready. Let the good news of the kingdom be preached to all the nations. Rescue all who can be rescued. Come and take Your rightful place in this world gone astray!" We long to see more of Your wonderful plan invade our lives and also Your entire world. But more than that, we long to see You! We are thankful that there is a blessing for those who believe without seeing, but we long for our eyes to see the King in all His beauty and majesty. Yes, Lord, let Your kingdom come!

35. Come, Lord Jesus, Come

Come, Lord Jesus, come
Establish Your kingdom
Come now and rule in this place

Come now and rule by Your grace
Come, Lord Jesus, come
Establish Your kingdom
Come even now as we sing
Come and be King

We welcome You, Lord Jesus
We welcome You as our King
We welcome You, Lord Jesus
Rule over everything

36. Specific Statements of His Will

Heavenly Father, today I want to state again that Your will is better than mine. It really is true that "Father knows best." Even though I don't know all of what Your will is for me today, I embrace it. However Your will becomes clear to me, I want to give myself fully to it. Make Your will known to me. Let me know what Your heart and desires are in the different settings I will be in today. And give me the grace to accomplish them.

Help me remember the specific statements of Your will from Your Word. Help me to walk in humility before You and those around me. Please help me to rejoice in all circumstances. Give me opportunity to speak up for those who cannot speak for themselves. Let all that I do today move toward the goal of seeing more people become genuine disciples of Jesus. Let me imitate You. Please live Your life through me!

37. The Greatest Expression of His Will

Father, since You said that all of Your other commandments are held up by the two love commandments, let me love better today than I did yesterday. Help me to freely give of myself for the highest good of others. Help me to do this with no strings attached. Let my love be as pure as possible. Help me love those who seem very lovable to me, and help me love those who seem very unlovable. Help me love those who are familiar to me and those who are unfamiliar to me as well. Let me see them through Your eyes and love them with Your love.

Help me grow in my love for You today. Remind me of the ways I already know how to love You, and help me accomplish them. And show me this day more or new ways to love You. Help me keep my eyes fixed on You so You can teach me to more fully obey this greatest commandment of Yours. Deepen my understanding, capacity, motivation, desire, and ability to love You more the way You deserve to be loved.

And since You said the only reason I have the capacity to love is because You have loved me, increase my awareness of Your unending and unfailing love for me. Please let me be a better receiver of Your love so I can be a better transmitter of it to You and others. Make my life a conduit for Your love. And keep it open and attached to Your sea of love.

38. On Earth As It Is In Heaven

Father, until Your kingdom comes fully, we will pray that it will come partially. Thank You for the assurance that we will go to heaven. But we also want to see more of heaven come to earth. We are grateful there still is a place where Your standard is upheld. But we want that standard to be upheld in the here and now as well. We are thankful that our sin has not tarnished Your home as it has tarnished ours. And we pray that You will remove as much stain as possible from our home. We are thankful that the place Jesus is preparing for us has not been ruined by our rebellion. And we now ask that both our rebellion and its consequences will be held in check.

Since Your name is still holy in heaven, Your kingdom is well established in heaven, and Your will is carried out fully in heaven, we pray that You would lay the template of heaven over this rough-cut earth—mark, cut, and trim us until what we see on earth is as close to heaven as it can possibly be in this present age. Let Your church lead the way. Let those of us who are bound for heaven be bound to live in a manner that reflects heaven. Help us to be as familiar with the way things work in our eternal home as we are with our temporary one. Lift our eyes so we can see Jesus there; help us to fix our eyes on Him; then turn us toward this world remembering what we have just seen.

39. Give Us

Father, when I come to these words of this prayer, they humble me. They tell me that I am desperately needy. They remind me of my spiritual poverty. They tell me that there are things I need that I cannot acquire on my own. I am not a self-made man, nor am I an island unto myself. They tell me that if these needs are going to be met, I must simply acknowledge them, come to You, and ask. I have no line of credit to draw on. I have no currency to offer You. I have no capacity to require anything from You. I can only come with my need. So here I am again, Lord, with nothing in my hand except my needs. Your Word is true when it says that apart from You I can do nothing. And apart from You I have nothing.

As I come, I come with confidence that because You have met my needs before, You will meet them again. I am thankful that when I come to you in this manner You never find fault with either me or my request. As I approach Your throne today, I acknowledge that I am not my own source. I come instead to the One who is the best and only true Source.

40. Give Us (2)

Heavenly Father, these words give me great hope because they not only tell me about my need; they also tell me about Your wonderful invitation. When I come before You with empty hands, I know that I am here because You have invited me to be here! I know I am not a bother or a beggar but a child who has come to the storehouse of the Father. I am so grateful that I am not an intrusion into Your busy schedule. Just as You have invited me into a relationship with You, You have also invited me to stay connected with You by daily coming to You with the most basic of requests. So, Father, it is good to be here again!

These words also give me hope because they tell me that You are the One who can supply my real needs. Thank You that my needs are not unmeetable. There is a place where I can go to have all of them met. Please continually remind me that they are not met outside of You. Every time I consider looking in another direction besides You, to have the needs of my life met, I ask You to gently but firmly remind me that You are the only Source of living water.

I bless You and worship You because You are both able and willing to meet all the needs I bring to You.

41. This Day

Father in heaven, I am so thankful for all the previous days. I am grateful for the relationship, the growth, the joy, the ministry, the forgiveness, and the memories of previous days. And I thank You for the anticipated tomorrows. Thank You that because You never change, I can anticipate more of life with You in the future. But today, I am thankful for this day. I ask that as You view this day it would be meaningful for You and Your purposes. This day, I want Your name to be more holy. This day, I want to see Your kingdom more established and expanded. This day I want more of Your will accomplished by me and through me. This day I want to take full advantage of Your wonderful supply. This day I want to revel in Your forgiveness and extend it to others. This day I want to follow Your leadership. And this day I want to run into the tower of Your strong name for protection.

Father I am grateful for these two words You included in this prayer. You were so wise to include them! They bring all of this prayer out of history and make it contemporary. They remind me of the daily nature of my relationship with You. They remind me that yesterday's manna was a wonderful meal but is now only a memory. They tell me that I need to stay current with You. So this day I come again to You through the use of this prayer.

42. This Day (2)

Father, I remember Joshua's challenge to the Israelites years ago. He challenged them to make a decision *this day* about who they were going to serve. I hear the same challenge to me today. This day I want to serve You! I remember making that life-altering decision years ago, and I renew it again today. I don't want anything or anyone else to be my lord and master. I want to serve You by serving those around me, but I don't want them to take Your unique place as Lord of my life.

And I remember the psalmist rejoicing in a day when the rejected stone became the chief cornerstone. Jesus, I also rejoice in this picture of Your exaltation. You deserve to be in that most important place. I remember when You were not the cornerstone of my life. Those days did not produce a lot of rejoicing. And I remember the day You became the most important stone of my life. I welcome You again today as my Chief Cornerstone. I ask that all of today's decisions would line up with You just like all the other stones are to line up with the chief cornerstone. If You catch me setting a stone that does not align with You, please check me and give me enough grace to realign it.

This day I choose You. This day I rejoice because You are the Chief Cornerstone.

43. Our Daily Bread—Physical Needs

You have been so faithful and consistent, Father, in providing for me and my family. You have provided all that we need and far more than we need. You have provided the physical needs we have been aware of and those we simply take for granted. You have provided not only food for us each day, but also our air, water, shelter, transportation, clothing, and more. When we have asked, You have provided. When we have not asked, You have still provided.

Though Your faithfulness has sometimes caused me to take You for granted, this day I determine to let Your faithfulness remind me that You are the Source of all my daily physical needs. You delight to meet these needs as I come and ask. Neither my freezer, my cupboard, my job, nor my bank account is my real source. You are the proper source to turn to, and today I turn to You to provide again these basic needs of my life.

44. Our Daily Bread—Nonphysical Needs

Father, it is so good to know that Your concern for us does not stop at our physical needs. I am grateful for this physical provision. But more than that, thanks that You provide for all our nonphysical needs as well. I have needs far beyond mere food, water, and shelter. Today I need and I ask for more of Your grace in my life. Today, I need more of that wisdom that comes down from You. I need more boldness and honesty to face situations and people and respond as Jesus would. I need the fruit of Your Spirit flowing through my life. I need Your love, joy, peace, patience, kindness, goodness, faithfulness, gentleness, and self-control to be growing and more evident in me. I need to learn from You how to have a gentle heart and walk in humility so my soul can find needed rest in You. I need the attitudes of the beatitudes to be more real in my life and responses. Lord, help me see my own spiritual poverty, mourn with those who mourn, walk in meekness, hunger and thirst for righteousness, be merciful, be a peacemaker, and undergo any persecution with joy.

Thank You that these things are all available to me when I come and ask. They are not too big for You to deal with. Thanks that You have answered this prayer in the past and that You will answer it in the future. Give me all that I need to live a full life that will bring honor and glory to Your name.

45. Our Daily Bread—Rations

Father, as I come to receive this wonderful daily bread today, I appreciate that it is freely given, but I also receive the responsibility that comes with another day's provisions. As a soldier in Your army, I pick up this MRE (meal ready to eat), and I also joyfully receive the "orders of the day" attached to it. I have plans for this day, which I believe are Your will, but You have complete authority to edit these plans and point me in a different direction. Lord, I yield any and all of my plans to a further understanding of Your moment-by-moment plans for me. Make me sensitive and aware of how You may want to communicate these plans to me. If You bring a person across my path I did not anticipate seeing today, and if there is a way You want me to minister to them, give me the ability to give more of You and Your life to them. If there is something You want me to receive from someone else that I did not expect to receive, give me grace to receive it. If there is a decision I need to make today that I did not anticipate making, allow me to make a kingdom-advancing decision.

Also, Lord, turn the daily bread I receive from You into holiness for Your name, advancement of Your kingdom, and accomplishment of Your will.

46. Our Daily Bread—Manna

In receiving Your daily bread today, Father, I remember that You said You gave daily bread to the Israelites in the wilderness to teach them that man needs much more than bread to live. In order to live well, we must receive every word that comes from Your mouth. Today, more than the physical and nonphysical areas and more than the specific orders You have for me, I want to receive the nourishment of the "every word" that You have for me.

As I open Your Word today, give me ears to hear what Your Spirit may be saying to me. Give me that ability to understand Your Word in its historical setting and also to see how my life is like that historical setting. Let me understand what You said to them and also what You are saying to me. I ask that Your Word would be alive and active in my heart and life today. Let it do its work in me. Let it cut what needs to be cut, restore what needs to be restored, tear down what needs to be torn down, build up what needs to be built up, correct what needs to be corrected, and teach me and instruct me in the way I should go. Remind me of things You have taught me in the past, and teach me new things I will need for today and beyond.

And then let me hear Your voice in any other means You choose to speak. Let me hear You through the voices of other people, through the Spirit-directed thoughts that come to my mind, as well as through the circumstances around me. Let me recognize Your voice in any way You would choose to speak. Help me to hear all that Your living Word and written Word have to say to me.

47. Our Daily Bread—Jesus

Heavenly Father, You are so generous in Your provision! You consistently give us all that we need in the physical and nonphysical realm. You graciously tell us Your plans and feed us from Your Word. But this morning, I am aware that the ultimate question about the daily bread is not "*What* is our daily bread?" but "*Who* is our Daily Bread?" Father, I am so grateful that the most perfect provision You give us is Your precious Son! More than bread or grace or wisdom or traits or teachings, I need more of Jesus! Thank You for the invitation to come to You today and ask You for more of Him. Because You have invited me to come before Your throne and ask boldly, I do come and boldly ask You to give me more of Jesus Christ. I ask not simply that You would help me to learn more about Him and be more like Him; I am asking for more of Him. Remove anything in me You need to remove to give me more of Him.

I ask for more of His mind to be in my mind. I ask for more of His nature to be my nature. I ask that more of His heart would be my heart. And more of His motives would be my motives.

Because He is the "indescribable gift," my words run short of what I am asking. So please go beyond my words and give me more of Your dear Son!

48. *Forgive Us*

This morning, Father, I am grateful that Jesus came as a wonderful example, teacher, healer, friend of sinners, and leader. But more than anything else, I am thankful that He came to be my Savior. Thank You that He came to forgive my sins. Thank You that the sins of my past have not been simply moved off to the side, slipped down on Your docket, or pushed out of the way. They have been removed, as far as the east is from the west!

Help me recognize my sin as sin. Help me to see it as You see it. Please check me when I try to downplay it as something less than a terrible violation of Your perfect standards. Balance me out between thinking too little of it or too much of it. Help me see my sin as neither so small that it does not need to be forgiven nor so big that it can't be forgiven.

Thank You that there is a way for my current sins to be forgiven. Thanks that as I walk in the light, my sins are forgiven. Please keep me transparent before You, Lord. Let me live with a commitment to not try to hide anything from You, the One who sees everything! And thanks that when I don't live in the light, I can confess my sins and You forgive me. Show me the value of keeping short lists with You. And thanks for the gift of repentance. Thank You that when I need to turn around, You convict me of my sin and of the righteous steps I need to take. Then You give me the grace to be able to make the turn away from it and toward You. Help me to turn quickly and thoroughly. And, thank You that You call us to grant forgiveness to others. You are so good to give us the command and the opportunity to forgive as You forgive. Help me to recognize the opportunity, to remember the forgiveness I have received, and to extend that forgiveness to other sinners.

Thank You, Lord for Your willingness to actually and fully release me from my offensive violations of Your standards.

49. As We Forgive

As I pray this line, You remind me that I am to not only act like You, but to reflect Your character. You are a forgiver, and therefore You want me to forgive. I am seeing that this truth is not limited to this line. It is true for the line before it and the two lines after it as well. So, Father, because You are a giver, let me also be a giver. And because You are a leader, let me also be a leader. And please let me be a deliverer like You as well.

Let me see that all the things You have so graciously given to me, both physical and nonphysical, are still Yours and You may want me to be a channel of blessing to someone else who needs them. If Jesus laid it all down and did not even grasp onto His glory, please don't let me grasp onto anything either.

And help me to lead others away from sin and into righteousness by following You closely. Help my life to be a light to show them where to walk and how to live. Keep my eyes fixed upon You as the guide and my feet following You closely so as others see my life, they will know where they should step.

And help me cooperate with You as You deliver more and more people from the evil one and all of his schemes. As You take my hand and rescue me when I am off the path, help me to reach out with my other hand so others can come with me back onto Your good path.

50. As We Forgive (2)
Father, today I ask You to help me catch the seriousness of this line. Let me see the real weight of this little word *as*. Father, I need Your grace, because I tend to think that the sins others commit against me are worse than the sins I commit against You or them. I need to be corrected and see that my sin against You, which You have so freely forgiven, is really far worse than any sin ever committed against me. So, Father, though it scares me to pray it, please do forgive me *as* I forgive others.

Help me to clearly understand how serious You are about this. Help me to understand Jesus' clear words on this topic without watering them down or making them weaker than they were when He said them. And, frankly, I need Your help to grant forgiveness. So give me the grace to take it step by step. Help me to recognize that I have been sinned against without this thought blowing me out of the water. Then help me remember the cross as the solution to this sin, just as it was the solution to my sin. Then allow me to fully release this sinner, just as You fully released me. And give me words and thoughts to bless them instead of my natural inclination to curse them. Finally, help me to remember the act of forgiveness and reapply it as many times as I need to until my feelings catch up with the reality of this prayer.

51. Lead Us

Father, You are the best leader ever! You lead from a perspective I don't have. You see over the next hill, and You see the entire path. Your leadership is one of the ways You demonstrate Your love to us. I am thankful. If I had led my life, it would have been far different, far less than it is. Your leadership has never taken me to a place that was bad for me to go. In fact, Your leadership has always led me toward Jesus.

At the beginning of Your ministry and also at the end of Your ministry, You called Peter to follow You. I hear Your voice calling me to do the same. Your Spirit has invited Your followers to keep in step with Him. He has said that His leadership in our lives is part of the evidence that we are Your children. Jesus has invited those who were weary to be yoked with Him. Thanks that You are giving me the same invitation today. I accept it!

Help me respond well to Your wonderful leadership. Help me see where You are going and move with You. Help me to not second-guess You. Remind me that You can lead me far better than I can lead You.

And also, thanks that You are not only the leader; You are the destination. Since You lead people into a closer, more fulfilling, more dependent life with You, please lead on!

52. Lead Us Not

When I come to this line in this prayer, Father, I recognize again what it teaches me about Your heart and the nature of prayer. You do not want me to be tempted, and You ask me to join You in this desire through prayer. Thank You that Your purpose is to draw me closer to You, not further away. You want me to be fulfilled in You, not in things less than You. I praise You because You are good through and through. And I ask that You would not let me be deceived into thinking anything less than this.

When I am tempted, it is not from You but rather from my own evil desire to live independently from You. And You are so good that even though You don't tempt me, You still make a way of escape when I am tempted. Let me recognize any temptation early on. Let me see clearly Your way of escape. Show me Jesus in the midst of the temptation, and give me the grace to follow Him at that moment.

In contrast to the schemes of the evil one to lead me away from You, please turn his efforts around on him, and cause them to draw me closer to You. Give me Your pure desires. And I ask that Jesus would take those desires, present Your truth to me in ways I can receive, and germinate it in me so that it produces more of Your life.

53. Lead Us Not (2)

Father, in this business of dealing with temptation, give me the needed discipline to cooperate with You. You have shown me the value of Your Word and of prayer in my fight to follow You. Please train me in the use of these two weapons. Increase my desire to pray, and increase the effectiveness of my prayers. And increase my desire to understand and apply Your Word to my life.

Make me more like Jesus in these two areas. As He was so skilled in the use of Your Word against the evil one, give me the discipline to be in Your Word and Your Word to be in me regularly. Make me hungry and thirsty for more of You. Let that hunger and thirst be fulfilled as I know You through Your Word. Tutor me in prayer so that I pray much more as Jesus prayed. Help me to see an increase in the amount and depth of my times of prayer. Show me more of the prayer life of Jesus. Show me how He prayed, how much He prayed, and why He prayed. And then please give me the discipline and the grace to have my prayer life reflect His prayer life.

Father, since I know this is Your will, I pray with confidence that these things will be accomplished. Remind me regularly of this prayer, and show me both the path and the progress. And, ultimately, show me more victory over sin and Satan because of it.

54. Deliver Us

Thank You, Father, that You are heavenly. You have a different perspective of the evil one than I do. From my perspective, there are times when it looks as though he has a chance to win. But I rejoice that from Your perspective, he is completely defeated! Today I want to further enter into the victory You have accomplished. I want to see more deliverance in my life and defeat in his life.

I do recognize that, even when I want to follow You well, it doesn't always happen. I know that I need Your deliverance even when I don't know I have strayed from Your path. Deliverer, keep Your eye on this wanderer. Shepherd, please care for this sheep.

Whether my wanderings have been intentional or unintentional, be both firm and gentle, and get me back to the green pastures and quiet waters You have prepared for me.

Father, I pray that every time You deliver me, I will learn. I want to learn the value of following You, and I want to learn the danger of not following You so that the next time I face a similar situation, I will stay yoked with You and not need as much deliverance.

55. Deliver Us (2)

Father, today, I praise You for Your complete victory over the evil one. Jesus, thank You for Your willingness to face this personification of evil so I do not have to. Today I ask for two things. First, I ask that You would not let me forget that he really is ultimate evil, and I ask that You would not let me forget that You are the ultimate Deliverer.

Father, I ask that You would deliver me from the evil one. Deliver me from his temptations to be satisfied with something less than a deep, growing relationship with You. And deliver me from the delusion that I can get there without desperate dependence on You. Deliver me from his subtle but serious attacks to relax, and deliver me from his front-on guerrilla warfare.

Fix my eyes so that they are always on Jesus. Train me in the use of the weapons of Your Word and prayer. Let me put on all the armor of God so that I can stand against the evil one this day and every day.

When I experience some measure of success, deliver me from any thoughts that it was the result of my doing. When I experience some measure of failure, deliver me from any thoughts that You will never be able to use me again.

And because I have prayed according to Your will, I thank You for how You will answer this prayer.

56. For the Kingdom and the Power and the Glory Belong to You

Heavenly Father, thank You for the confidence You give us when we pray. As we come to this line, we come with assurance because the purpose of our prayers has been to see more of heaven come to earth. We are assured that You, as the King, will bring Your kingdom. We also have confidence because we are not expecting these prayers to be answered based on any sense of power we have, but because You have all power. And You use that power wisely. We have confidence because as we have prayed; we have not sought to bring any glory to ourselves, but only to You. You know how to handle glory; we don't!

So, Lord, for the sake of Your kingdom, based on Your power, and in order for You to receive more glory, we say, "Amen, and amen!" Let it be!

Afterword
For Better or for Worse

In his book, *Praying Like Jesus,* James Mulholland likens praying the Lord's Prayer to making a marriage vow. Marilyn and I have been married for many wonderful years. Our wedding ceremony lasted about forty-five minutes. Sharing our vows took less than two minutes. Praying this prayer is like standing before the altar with my wife: The vows and the prayer take a short time to pray, but unless the vows and the prayer are lived out for years to come, they are neither meaningful nor fulfilled.

One day, as Jesus saw a crowd gathering, He went up to the side of a hill and began to teach them. Matthew recorded these words in what we call the Sermon on the Mount, in Matthew 5–7. Jesus concluded this series of teachings with a very interesting story. Many of us sang about this story as kids. Do you remember the song? "The wise man built his house upon the rock..." It deserves a closer look at this point in our journey.

> *"Therefore everyone who hears these words of mine and puts them into practice is like a wise man who built his house on the rock. The rain came down, the streams rose, and the winds blew and beat against that house; yet it did not fall, because it had its foundation on the rock. But everyone who hears these words of mine and does not put them into practice is like a foolish man who built his house on sand.*

The rain came down, the streams rose, and the winds blew and beat against that house, and it fell with a great crash." (Matthew 7:24–27)

Notice several things about this short story. Everyone who hears Jesus' words is building a house. The location of the foundation of that house is either on the rock or on sand and reflects either wisdom or foolishness. Severe weather conditions are going to come to both houses. When they come, one house will not fall, and the other house will fall with a great crash. The point of this story is clear. Whether the weather destroys the house or the house remains standing is determined by only one thing: not *if* they hear Jesus' words, but *how they respond* to Jesus' words. One man *puts them into practice*. His house stands. The other man *does not put them into practice*. His house falls.

This book is based upon the words of the Lord's Prayer recorded in Matthew 6:9–13. These are some of the exact words Jesus had in mind when He spoke the story in Matthew 7:24–27. Hearing the words does not secure the house. Liking the words does not secure the house. Reading a book and understanding more about the words does not secure the house. In fact, hearing the words of Jesus could make your life worse rather than better! The only thing that will cause the house to be secure in the midst of coming storms is putting the words into practice.

So although my desire is that as you have worked through this book, your life—your prayer life and your entire life—will become better, there is the possibility of it becoming worse. The outcome will depend entirely upon what you do now with Jesus' words. If you put them into practice, it will be stronger. It will be better. If you don't, it will become worse.

So I invite you to be wise. I invite you to build a house with a strong and secure foundation. I invite you to practice these words for about the next fifty years and see how it works out.

The Debt of Love I Owe

Based upon Romans 13:8, it is very appropriate for me to acknowledge the debt of love I owe to the following people, as they have helped me not simply write this book but also live more like the Lord's Prayer:

For "test driving" this material and helping make it more practical—the people and leadership of Peninsula Christian Fellowship, Grace Foursquare Church, and Calvary Community Church, specifically Kurt, Dave, and Scott, as well as a host of other ministry friends.

For essential work in helping with and honing the details of the publication process—Don and Jenni from D. C. Jacobson and Associates.

For being the best family ever—Marilyn, Josh and Kara, Sean and Angela, Keven and Andrea, and Joseph. And the next generation—Austin and Ian, Merilee and Solomon, Giuseppe and Gianna, and Ethan.

And most of all, for being the best possible Teacher, Friend, and Savior—the Lord Jesus Christ!

Now It's Your Turn...

If this book has helped you draw closer to Jesus, if it has assisted you in your prayer journey, if you think it can help the bride become more beautiful, don't keep this to yourself! Here are some things you can do to pass it on and expand our community of pray-ers:

- Share the book with others. As you read the book, did names come to your mind of people who should read it? If so, encourage them to go to the Web site and order a copy. Or order copies for them and others as gifts. Quantity discounts are available.

- Visit *www.livingprayer.net* and tell us how *Living Prayer* has affected you. Go to the "Stories" page and fill out the form.

- Post a review on Amazon.com. These reviews make a difference.

- If you are interested in leading a group study through this material, a carefully written study guide is available as a free download at the Web site. Contact us and ask for one.

- On our Web site there are many related articles that will help you continue to understand and grow in prayer. Read, download, and share these with others.

- Add a link from your Web site to *www.livingprayer.net* or blog about *Living Prayer* and share it with your social network.

- Become a Facebook friend of *Living Prayer*. We will confirm you as a friend and keep you posted on news and other items related to *Living Prayer*.

- If you would like to have Dennis come share on this topic with your congregation or group, he is an experienced and gifted communicator and would be happy to consider your request. Contact him through the web site or at dennisfuqua@gmail.com.

About the Author

Dennis Fuqua (pronounced few-kway) has been the director of International Renewal Ministries (www.prayersummits.net) since 2000. Prior to that, he pastored for twenty-five years in Gig Harbor, Washington. In 1989, IRM (under the direction of Dr. Joe Aldrich) gave birth to the Pastors' Prayer Summit movement. Now Dennis helps shepherd this movement, which has spread to at least forty states and nearly thirty nations. He not only facilitates Prayer Summits for pastors in cities, but also for congregations. He speaks often on topics related to both individual and corporate prayer in congregations, conferences, and retreats. His passion is to see the church relate best to God, to itself, and to those who have not yet placed their faith in Jesus Christ. He is a member of America's National Prayer Committee and Mission America Coalition. Dennis and his wife, Marilyn, live in Vancouver, Washington. He loves the Pacific Northwest, playing golf, watching sports, late sixties music, God, and being with his family, though not necessarily in that order.

LIVING PRAYER:
The Lord's Prayer Alive *in* You

After nearly 30 years of using the pattern of the Lord's Prayer for his own personal life, Dennis Fuqua has not only written the book, ***Living Prayer; the Lord's Prayer Alive in You***, but has also developed this **companion seminar** to help us really grasp the significance and use of this simple but profound prayer. Just as the Lord communicated with His people through the Written Word and the Living Word, so also, we want to communicate this essential message in a written way and in a personal way.

The ***Living Prayer Seminar*** is not a series of sermons pieced together. It is a highly interactive, fun, creative time which will help you not only know and appreciate this most well-known prayer, but also gain experience and confidence in praying it.

With 25 years of pastoral ministry and the experience of leading an international prayer ministry since 2000, Dennis finds a wonderful balance of sharing what he has gleaned from this prayer and helping you glean for yourself.

You will leave this seminar with a greater freshness in your own prayer life and the ability to share with others how they can glean from this "best-of-all prayers from the Best-of-all Pray-ers."

Contact us for more information:

livingprayerbook@gmail.com
www.livingprayer.net
17221 SE 23rd Drive
Vancouver, WA 98683

A few comments from those who have attended a *Living Prayer Seminar* ...

This seminar stopped me dead in my tracks! I found myself prostrate before the Lord—something I've never done, I'm sorry to admit. This has changed my life forever. —Bev

My eyes have truly been opened to what the Lord expects from me. Thank you so very much for what you do. —James

This seminar has been tremendous. I have never thought about how much the Lord's Prayer should be used as our guide to effective praying. After the first day, it has changed my prayer life. I appreciated the very practical suggestions and how we can do this on a daily basis. —Darlene

The Lord's Prayer has become very deep for me and a treasure to be mined. Prior to this (seminar), they were simply words to me. —Judi

We have been so blessed by the *Living Prayer Seminar* we attended earlier this year. It has changed the way both of us pray and think about prayer. You equipped us with tools and teaching that have allowed us to deepen our relationship with the Father, Son, and Holy Spirit. —Tyler and Kim

Now I'm getting a glimpse of what this prayer really means. This seminar has opened up a whole new meaning of this prayer. I hope to be a living testimony of this prayer. This has converted me to be a disciple of this prayer. —Dave

Very encouraging! I'm excited to try this way of praying; now the Lord's Prayer means so much more to me. —Jennifer

This was such a wonderful way to refresh my prayer life. —Shawndra

And from a few pastors who hosted a seminar ...

Both the material presented during the *Living Prayer Seminar* and the presenter have had a profound impact on our congregation. Dennis' whimsical, humorous, and very biblical approach to the subject of prayer spoke to the hearts of our people and is moving us to pray more "biblically." —Pastor Tom, WA

This seminar was fast-moving, fun, insightful, biblical and very encouraging. I heard things about how to pray that I've never heard or read anywhere before, and I have a shelf of books on prayer. I will never pray the same way again. —Pastor Steve, MA

This book and the seminar have opened my eyes and revolutionized my prayer life as well as that of my congregation. In the past, (the Lord's Prayer) was used like a dead, formal mantra. I have come to value it as never before. —Pastor Tim, WA

I gained a new appreciation for the importance of the Lord's Prayer and new insights on how to use this prayer as a basis for my own praying. —Pastor Philip, RI